The Crash of 2008

and What it Means

The Age of Fallibility: The Consequences of the War on Terror

The Bubble of American Supremacy: The Cost of Bush's War in Iraq

George Soros on Globalization

Open Society: Reforming Global Capitalism

The Crisis of Global Capitalism: Open Society Endangered

Soros on Soros: Staying Ahead of the Curve

Underwriting Democracy

Opening the Soviet System

The Alchemy of Finance: Reading the Mind of the Market

GEORGE SOROS

The Crash of 2008 and What it Means

THE NEW PARADIGM FOR FINANCIAL MARKETS

PublicAffairs

NEW YORK

TEXT SET IN JANSON TEXT

Library of Congress Cataloging-in-Publication Data
Soros, George.
 The new paradigm for financial markets : the credit crisis of 2008 and what it means / George Soros.
  p. cm.
 ISBN 978–1–58648–683–9 (hardcover : alk. paper) —
 ISBN 978–1–58648–684–6 (electronic book) 1. Financial crises—United States. 2. United States—Economic policy. 3. United States—Economic conditions—21st century. 4. Credit—United States. I. Title.
HB3722.S673 2008
 332.0973—dc22

                                                          2008013695
           ISBN 978–1–58648–699–0 (paperback)
       ISBN 978–0–78674–493–0 (electronic book, paperback edition)
                 3 5 7 9 10 8 6 4 2

Contents

Part One: Perspective

Part Two: The Current Crisis and Beyond

Part Three: The Crash of 2008 and What it Means

Preface to the
Paperback Edition

This book puts forward a conceptual framework for understanding human affairs in general and financial markets in particular. I have been working on it all my life but it is only now that the framework has gained some recognition because not only did it explain the Crash of 2008 but more or less predicted how it would happen. I say "more or less" because when I said that "we are in the midst of the worst financial crisis since the 1930s," I did not anticipate that as a consequence of Lehman Brother's bankruptcy on September 15, 2008, the financial system would actually break down. Most of this book was written at the end of 2007 and the beginning of 2008. It was first published as an electronic book and then as a hardcover later in the spring. That version is reproduced here in its original form with only a few clarifications and improvements which are printed in italics. I am doing this to preserve the historical accuracy of the text. I have also added an additional section, Part Three: The Crash of 2008 and What it Means, intended to bring the book and my argument up to date.

Introduction

We are in the midst of the worst financial crisis since the 1930s. In some ways it resembles other crises that have occurred in the last twenty-five years, but there is a profound difference: the current crisis marks the end of an era of credit expansion based on the dollar as the international reserve currency. The periodic crises were part of a larger boom-bust process; the current crisis is the culmination of a super-boom that has lasted for more than twenty-five years.

To understand what is going on we need a new paradigm. The currently prevailing paradigm, namely that financial markets tend towards equilibrium, is both false and misleading; our current troubles can be largely attributed to the fact that the international financial system has been developed on the basis of that paradigm.

The new paradigm I am proposing *differs from the old one in two important respects. First, I contend that financial markets never reflect the underlying reality accurately; they* always *distort it in some way or another and the distortions find expression in market prices. Second, those distortions can,* occasionally, *find ways to affect the fundamentals that market prices are supposed to reflect.*

My conceptual framework is not confined to the financial markets. It deals with the relationship between thinking and reality, and it claims that misconceptions and misinterpretations play a major role in shaping the course of history. I started developing this framework as a student at the London School of Economics before I became active in the financial markets. As I have written before, I was greatly influenced by the philosophy of Karl Popper, and this made me question the assumptions on which the theory of perfect competition is based, in particular the assumption of perfect knowledge. I came to realize that market participants cannot base their decisions on knowledge alone, and their biased perceptions have ways of influencing not only market prices but also the fundamentals that those prices are supposed to reflect. I argued that the participants' thinking plays a dual function. On the one hand, they seek to understand their situation. I called this the cognitive function. On the other hand, they try to change the situation. I called this the participating or manipulative function. The two functions work in opposite directions and, under certain circumstances, they can interfere with each other. I called this interference reflexivity.

When I became a market participant, I applied my conceptual framework to the financial markets. It allowed me to gain a better understanding of initially self-reinforcing but eventually self-defeating boom-bust processes, and I put that insight to good use as the manager of a hedge fund. I expounded the theory of reflexivity in my first book, *The Alchemy of Finance*, which was published in 1987. The book acquired a cult following, but the theory of reflexivity was not taken seriously in academic circles. I myself harbored grave doubts about whether I was saying something new and significant. After all, I was dealing with one of the most basic and most thoroughly studied problems of philosophy, and everything that could be said on the subject had probably already been said. Nevertheless, my conceptual framework remained something very important for me personally. It guided me both in making money as a hedge fund manager and in spending it as a philanthropist, and it became an integral part of my identity.

When the financial crisis erupted, I had retired from actively managing my fund, having previously changed its status from an aggressive hedge fund to a more sedate endowment fund. The crisis forced me, however, to refocus my attention on the financial markets, and I became more actively engaged in making investment decisions. Then, towards the end of 2007, I decided to write a book analyzing and explaining the current situation. I was motivated by three considerations. First, a new paradigm was urgently needed for a better understanding of what is going on. Second, engaging in a serious study could help me in my investment decisions. Third, by providing a timely insight into the financial markets, I would ensure that the theory of reflexivity would finally receive serious consideration. It is difficult to gain attention for an abstract theory, but people are intensely interested in the financial markets, especially when they are in turmoil. I have already used the financial markets as a laboratory for testing the theory of reflexivity in *The Alchemy of Finance*; the current situation provides an excellent opportunity to demonstrate its relevance and importance. Of the three considerations, the third weighed most heavily in my decision to publish this book.

The fact that I had more than one objective in writing it makes the book more complicated than it would be if it were focused solely on the unfolding financial crisis. Let me explain briefly how the theory of reflexivity applies to the crisis. Contrary to classical economic theory, which assumes perfect knowledge, neither market participants nor the monetary and fiscal authorities can base their decisions purely on knowledge. Their misjudgments and misconceptions affect market prices, and, more importantly, market prices affect the so-called fundamentals that they are supposed to reflect. Market prices do not deviate from a theoretical equilibrium in a random manner, as the current paradigm holds. Participants' and regulators' views never correspond to the actual state of affairs; that is to say, markets never reach the equilibrium postulated by economic theory. There is a two-way reflexive connection between perception and reality which can give rise to initially self-reinforcing but eventually self-defeating boom-bust processes, or bubbles. *As we shall see, bubbles are not the only form in which reflexivity manifests itself in financial markets, but they are the most dramatic and they can have disastrous consequences. Bubbles are often responsible for financial crises and play an important role in the evolution of the regulatory regime. Thus they deserve special attention.*

Every bubble consists of a trend that can be observed in the real world and a misconception relating to that trend. The two elements interact with each other in a reflexive manner. There has been a bubble in the U.S. housing market, but the current crisis is not merely the bursting of the housing bubble. It is bigger than the periodic financial crises we have experienced in our lifetime. All those crises are part of what I call a super-bubble—a long-term reflexive process which has evolved over the last twenty-five years or so. It consists of a prevailing trend, credit expansion, and a prevailing misconception, market fundamentalism (aka *laissez-faire* in the nineteenth century), which holds that markets should be given free rein. The previous crises served as successful tests which reinforced the prevailing trend and the prevailing misconception. The current crisis constitutes the turning point when both the trend and the misconception have become unsustainable.

All this needs a lot more explanation. The explanation employs four levels of abstraction, in descending order. On the most abstract level, I explore the relationship between thinking and reality and introduce the concept of reflexivity. On the next level, I apply that concept to the financial markets. Then I focus on one particular manifestation of reflexivity, namely bubbles. Finally, I propose a specific hypothesis relating to the current moment of history. I contend that more than one bubble is involved. The bursting of the U.S. housing bubble served as a detonator that set off a much larger explosion: the bursting of a super-bubble that has been growing since the 1980s. The U.S housing bubble is relatively simple; the super-bubble is much more complicated. It will be explored at some length in Part 2. After setting the stage, I devote the first part of this book to the theory of reflexivity, which goes well beyond the financial markets. People interested solely in the current crisis will find it hard going, but those who make the effort will, I hope, find it rewarding. It constitutes my main interest, my life's work. Readers of my previous books will note that I have repeated some passages from them because the points I am making remain the same. Part 2 draws both on the conceptual framework and on my practical experience as a hedge fund manager to illuminate the current situation.

Setting the Stage

The outbreak of the current financial crisis can be officially fixed as August 2007. That was when the central banks had to intervene to provide liquidity to the banking system. As the BBC reported:*

- On August 6, American Home Mortgage, one of the largest U.S. independent home loan providers, filed for bankruptcy after laying off the majority of its staff. The company said it was a victim of the slump in the U.S. housing market that had caught out many subprime borrowers and lenders.
- On August 9, short-term credit markets froze up after a large French bank, BNP Paribas, suspended three of its investment funds worth 2 billion euros, citing problems in the U.S. subprime mortgage sector. BNP said it could not value the assets in the funds because the market had disappeared. The European Central Bank pumped 95 billion euros into the eurozone banking system to ease the subprime credit crunch. The U.S. Federal Reserve and the Bank of Japan took similar steps.

*BBC News, "Timeline: Sub-Prime losses: How Did the Sub-Prime Crisis Unfold?" http://news.bbc.co.uk/1/hi/business/7096845.stm.

- On August 10, the European Central Bank provided an extra 61 billion euros of funds for banks. The U.S. Federal Reserve said it would provide as much overnight money as would be needed to combat the credit crunch.
- On August 13, the European Central Bank pumped 47.7 billion euros into the money markets, its third cash injection in as many working days. Central banks in the United States and Japan also topped up earlier injections. Goldman Sachs said it would pump 3 billion dollars into a hedge fund hit by the credit crunch to shore up its value.
- On August 16, Countrywide Financial, the largest U.S. mortgage originator, drew down its entire 11.5 billion dollar credit line. Australian mortgage lender Rams also admitted liquidity problems.
- On August 17, the U.S. Federal Reserve cut the discount rate (the interest rate at which it lends to banks) by a half a percentage point to help banks deal with credit problems. (But it did not help. Subsequently the central banks of the developed world ended up injecting funds on a larger scale for longer periods and accepting a wider range of securities as collateral than ever before in history.)
- On September 13, it was disclosed that Northern Rock (the largest British mortgage banker) was bordering on insolvency (which triggered an old-fashioned bank run—for the first time in Britain in a hundred years).

The crisis was slow in coming, but it could have been anticipated several years in advance. It had its origins in the bursting of the Internet bubble in late 2000. The Fed responded by cutting the federal funds rate from 6.5 percent to

3.5 percent within the space of just a few months. Then came the terrorist attack of September 11, 2001. To counteract the disruption of the economy, the Fed continued to lower rates—all the way down to 1 percent by July 2003, the lowest rate in half a century, where it stayed for a full year. For thirty-one consecutive months the base inflation-adjusted short-term interest rate was negative.

Cheap money engendered a housing bubble, an explosion of leveraged buyouts, and other excesses. When money is free, the rational lender will keep on lending until there is no one else to lend to. Mortgage lenders relaxed their standards and invented new ways to stimulate business and generate fees. Investment banks on Wall Street developed a variety of new techniques to hive credit risk off to other investors, like pension funds and mutual funds, which were hungry for yield. They also created structured investment vehicles (SIVs) to keep their own positions off their balance sheets.

From 2000 until mid-2005, the market value of existing homes grew by more than 50 percent, and there was a frenzy of new construction. Merrill Lynch estimated that about half of all American GDP growth in the first half of 2005 was housing related, either directly, through home building and housing-related purchases like new furniture, or indirectly, by spending the cash generated from the refinancing of mortgages. Martin Feldstein, a former chairman of the Council of Economic Advisers, estimated that from 1997 through 2006, consumers drew more than $9 trillion in cash out of their home equity. A 2005 study led by Alan Greenspan estimated that in the 2000s, home equity withdrawals were financing 3 percent of all personal consumption. By the first quarter of 2006, home equity extraction made up nearly 10 percent of disposable personal income.*

Double-digit price increases in house prices engendered speculation. When the value of property is expected to rise more than the cost of borrowing, it makes sense to own more property than one wants to occupy. By 2005, 40 percent of all homes purchased were not meant to serve as permanent residences but as investments or second homes.† Since growth in real median income was anemic in the 2000s, lenders strained ingenuity to make houses appear affordable. The most popular devices were adjustable rate mortgages (ARMs) with "teaser," below-market initial rates for an initial two-year period. It was assumed that after two years, when the higher rate kicked in, the mortgage would be refinanced, taking advantage of the higher prices and generating a new set of fees for the lenders. Credit standards collapsed, and mortgages were made widely available to people with low credit ratings (called subprime mortgages), many of whom were well-to-do. "Alt-A" (or liar loans), with low or no documentation, were common, including, at the extreme, "ninja" loans (no income, no job, no assets), frequently with the active connivance of the mortgage brokers and mortgage lenders.

*_Economist_, September 10, 2005; Martin Feldstein, "Housing, Credit Markets and the Business Cycle," National Bureau of Economic Research working paper 13,471, October 2007; Alan Greenspan and James Kennedy, "Estimates of Home Mortgage Origination, Repayments, and Debts on One- to Four-Family Residences," Federal Reserve staff working paper 2005–41 (data updated through 2007 by Dr. Kennedy and furnished to the author).

†Joseph R. Mason and Joshua Rosner, "How Resilient Are Mortgage Backed Securities to Collateralized Debt Obligation Market Disruption?" paper presented at the Hudson Institute, Washington, D.C., February 15, 2007, 11.

Banks sold off their riskiest mortgages by repackaging them into securities called collateralized debt obligations (CDOs). CDOs channeled the cash flows from thousands of mortgages into a series of tiered, or tranched, bonds with risks and yields tuned to different investor tastes. The top-tier tranches, which comprised perhaps 80 percent of the bonds, would have first call on all underlying cash flows, so they could be sold with a AAA rating. The lower tiers absorbed first-dollar risks but carried higher yields. In practice, the bankers and the rating agencies grossly underestimated the risks inherent in absurdities like ninja loans.

Securitization was meant to reduce risks through risk tiering and geographic diversification. As it turned out, they increased the risks by transferring ownership of mortgages from bankers who knew their customers to investors who did not. Instead of a bank or savings and loan approving a credit and retaining it on its books, loans were sourced by brokers; temporarily "'warehoused" by thinly capitalized "mortgage bankers"; then sold en bloc to investment banks, who manufactured the CDOs, which were rated by ratings agencies and sold off to institutional investors. All income from the original sourcing through the final placement was fee based—the higher the volumes, the bigger the bonuses. The prospect of earning fees without incurring risks encouraged lax and deceptive business practices. The subprime area, which dealt with inexperienced and uninformed customers, was rife with fraudulent activities. The word "teaser rates" gave the game away.

Starting around 2005, securitization became a mania. It was easy and fast to create "synthetic" securities that mimicked the risks of real securities but did not carry the expense of buying and assembling actual loans. Risky paper could therefore be multiplied well beyond the actual supply in the market. Enterprising investment bankers sliced up CDOs and repackaged them into CDOs of CDOs, or CDO^{2}s. There were even CDO^{3}s. The highest slices of lower-rated CDOs obtained AAA ratings. In this way more AAA liabilities were created than there were AAA assets. Towards the end, synthetic products accounted for more than half the trading volume.

The securitization mania was not confined to mortgages and spread to other forms of credit. By far the largest synthetic market is constituted by credit default swaps (CDSs). This arcane synthetic financial instrument was invented in Europe in the early 1990s. Early CDSs were customized agreements between two banks. Bank A, the swap seller (protection purchaser), agreed to pay an annual fee for a set period of years to Bank B, the swap buyer (protection seller), with respect to a specific portfolio of loans. Bank B would commit to making good Bank A's losses on portfolio defaults during the life of the swap. Prior to CDSs, a bank wishing to diversify its portfolio would need to buy or sell pieces of loans, which was complicated because it required the permission of the borrower; consequently, this form of diversification became very popular. Terms were standardized, and the notional value of the contracts grew to about a trillion dollars by 2000.

Hedge funds entered the market in force in the early 2000s. Specialized credit hedge funds effectively acted as unlicensed insurance companies, collecting premiums on the CDOs and other securities that they insured. The value of the insurance was often questionable because contracts could be assigned without notifying the counterparties. The market grew exponentially until it came to overshadow all other markets in nominal terms. The estimated nominal value of CDS contracts outstanding is $42.6 trillion. To put matters in perspective, this is equal to almost the entire household wealth of the United States. The capitalization of the U.S. stock market is $18.5 trillion, and the U.S. treasuries market is only $4.5 trillion.

The securitization mania led to an enormous increase in the use of leverage. To hold ordinary bonds requires a margin of 10 percent; synthetic bonds created by credit default swaps can be traded on a margin of 1.5 percent. This allowed hedge funds to show good profits by exploiting risk differentials on a leveraged basis, driving down risk premiums.

It was bound to end badly. There was a precedent to go by. The market in collateralized mortgage obligations (CMOs) started to develop in the 1980s. In 1994, the market in the lowest-rated tranches—or "toxic waste," as they were known—blew up when a $2 billion hedge fund could not meet a margin call, leading to the demise of Kidder Peabody and total losses of about $55 billion. But no regulatory action was taken. Former Federal Reserve governor Edward M. Gramlich privately warned Federal Reserve Chairman Alan Greenspan about abusive behavior in the subprime mortgage markets in 2000, but the warning was swept aside. Gramlich went public with his worries in 2007 and published a book on the subprime bubble just before the crisis first broke. Charles Kindleberger, an expert on bubbles, warned of the housing bubble in 2002. Martin Feldstein, Paul Volcker (former chairman of the Federal Reserve), and Bill Rhodes (a senior official of Citibank) all made bearish warnings. Nouriel Roubini predicted that the housing bubble would lead to a recession in 2006. But no one, including myself, anticipated how big the bubble could grow and how long it could last. As the *Wall Street Journal* recently noted, there were many hedge funds taking a bearish stance on housing, but "they suffered such painful losses waiting for a collapse" that most eventually gave up their positions.*

Signs of trouble started to multiply early in 2007. On February 22, HSBC fired the head of its U.S. mortgage lending business, recognizing losses reaching $10.8 billion. On March 9, DR Horton, the biggest U.S. homebuilder, warned of losses from subprime mortgages. On March 12, New Century Financial, one of the biggest subprime lenders, had its shares suspended from trading amid fears that the company was headed for bankruptcy. On March 13, it was reported that late payments on mortgages and home foreclosures rose to new highs. On March 16, Accredited Home Lenders Holding put up $2.7 billion of its subprime loan book for sale at a heavy discount to generate cash for business operations. On April 2, New Century Financial filed for Chapter 11 bankruptcy protection after it was forced to repurchase billions of dollars worth of bad loans.†

On June 15, 2007, Bear Stearns announced that two large mortgage hedge funds were having trouble meeting margin calls. Bear grudgingly created a $3.2 billion credit line to bail out one fund and let the other collapse. Investors' equity of $1.5 billion was mostly wiped out.

Wall Street Journal, February 27, 2008, and January 15, 2008; *New York Times*, October 26, 2007.

†"Bleak Housing Outlook for US Firm," *BBC News*, March 8, 2007, http://news.bbc.co.uk/2/hi/business/6429815.stm.

The failure of the two Bear Stearns mortgage hedge funds in June badly rattled the markets, but U.S. Federal Reserve Chairman Ben Bernanke and other senior officials reassured the public that the subprime problem was an isolated phenomenon. Prices stabilized, although the flow of bad news continued unabated. As late as July 20, Bernanke still estimated subprime losses at only about $100 billion. When Merrill Lynch and Citigroup took big write-downs on in-house collateralized debt obligations, the markets actually staged a relief rally. The S&P 500 hit a new high in mid-July.

It was only at the beginning of August that financial markets really took fright. It came as a shock when Bear Stearns filed for bankruptcy protection for two hedge funds exposed to subprime loans and stopped clients from withdrawing cash from a third fund. As mentioned, Bear Stearns had tried to save these entities by providing $3.2 billion of additional funding.

Once the crisis erupted, financial markets unraveled with remarkable rapidity. Everything that could go wrong did. A surprisingly large number of weaknesses were revealed in a remarkably short period of time. What started with low-grade subprime mortgages soon spread to CDOs, particularly those synthetic ones that were constructed out of the top slice of subprime mortgages. The CDOs themselves were not readily tradable, but there were tradable indexes representing the various branches. Investors looking for cover and short sellers looking for profits rushed to sell these indexes, and they declined precipitously, bringing the value of the various branches of CDOs that they were supposed to represent into question. Investment banks carried large positions of CDOs off balance sheet in so-called structured investment vehicles

(SIVs). The SIVs financed their positions by issuing asset-backed commercial paper. As the value of CDOs came into question, the asset-backed commercial paper market dried up, and the investment banks were forced to bail out their SIVs. Most investment banks took the SIVs into their balance sheets and were forced to recognize large losses in the process. Investment banks were also sitting on large loan commitments to finance leveraged buyouts. In the normal course of events, they would package these loans as collateralized loan obligations (CLOs) and sell them off, but the CLO market came to a standstill together with the CDO market, and the banks were left holding a bag worth about $250 billion. Some banks allowed their SIVs to go bust, and some reneged on their leveraged buyout obligations. This, together with the size of the losses incurred by the banks, served to unnerve the stock market, and price movements became chaotic. So-called market-neutral hedge funds, which exploit small discrepancies in market prices by using very high leverage, ceased to be market neutral and incurred unusual losses. A few highly leveraged ones were wiped out, damaging the reputation of their sponsors and unleashing lawsuits.

All this put tremendous pressure on the banking system. Banks had to put additional items on their balance sheets at a time when their capital base was impaired by unexpected losses. They had difficulty assessing their exposure and even greater difficulties estimating the exposure of their counterparts. Consequently they were reluctant to lend to each other and eager to hoard their liquidity. At first, central banks found it difficult to inject enough liquidity because commercial banks avoided using any of the facilities which had an onus attached to them, and they were also reluctant to deal with each other, but eventually these obstacles were overcome. After all, if there is one thing central banks know how to do, that is to provide liquidity. Only the Bank of England suffered a major debacle when it attempted to rescue Northern Rock, an overextended mortgage lender. Its rescue effort resulted in a run on the bank. Eventually Northern Rock was nationalized and its obligations added to the national debt, pushing the United Kingdom beyond the limits imposed by the Maastricht Treaty.

Although liquidity had been provided, the crisis refused to abate. Credit spreads continued to widen. Almost all the major banks—Citigroup, Merrill Lynch, Lehman Brothers, Bank of America, Wachovia, UBS, Credit Suisse—announced major write-downs in the fourth quarter, and most have signaled continued write-downs in 2008. Both AIG and Credit Suisse made preliminary fourth-quarter write-down announcements that they repeatedly revised, conveying the doubtless accurate impression that they had lost control of their balance sheets. A $7.2 billion trading fiasco at Société Générale announced on January 25, 2008, coincided with a selling climax in the stock market and an extraordinary 75 basis point cut in the federal funds rate eight days before the regularly scheduled meeting, when the rate was cut a further 50 basis points. This was unprecedented.

Distress spread from residential real estate to credit card debt, auto debt, and commercial real estate. Trouble at the monoline insurance companies, which traditionally specialized in municipal bonds but ventured into insuring structured and synthetic products, caused the municipal bond market to be disrupted. An even larger unresolved problem is looming in the credit default swaps market.

Over the past several decades the United States has weathered several major financial crises, like the international lending crisis of the 1980s and the savings and loan crisis of the early 1990s. But the current crisis is of an entirely different character. It has spread from one segment of the market to others, particularly those which employ newly created structured and synthetic instruments. Both the exposure and the capital base of the major financial institutions have been brought into question, and the uncertainties are likely to remain unresolved for an extended period of time. This is impeding the normal functioning of the financial system and is liable to have far-reaching consequences for the real economy.

Both the financial markets and the financial authorities have been very slow to recognize that the real economy is bound to be affected. It is hard to understand why this should be so. The real economy was stimulated by credit expansion. Why should it not be negatively affected by credit contraction? One cannot escape the conclusion that both the financial authorities and market participants harbor fundamental misconceptions about the way financial markets function. These misconceptions have manifested themselves not only in a failure to understand what is going on; they have given rise to the excesses which are at the root of the current market turmoil.

I shall argue that the global financial system has been built on false premises. This would be a shocking proposition except for the even more shocking proposition that misconceptions characterize not only financial markets but *all* human constructs.

In Part 1, I shall lay out the conceptual framework in terms of which the functioning of financial markets can be understood. In Part 2, I shall apply that framework to the present moment in history.

The Crash of 2008
and What it Means

PART I

Perspective

CHAPTER 1

The Core Idea

My starting point is that our understanding of the world in which we live is inherently imperfect because we are part of the world we seek to understand. There may be other factors that interfere with our ability to acquire knowledge of the natural world, but the fact that we are part of the world poses a formidable obstacle to the understanding of human affairs.

People with imperfect understanding interact with reality in two ways. On the one hand they seek to understand the world in which they live. I call this the cognitive function. On the other, people seek to make an impact on the world and change their situation to their advantage. I used to call this the participating function, but for some purposes I now consider it more appropriate to call it the manipulative function.* If the two functions were isolated from each other they could serve their purpose perfectly well: the participants' understanding could qualify as knowledge, and their actions

*Cognitive scientists call it the executive function. Aristotle called it practical reason to distinguish it from theoretical reason, which is the equivalent of the cognitive function.

could have the desired results. For this reason it is tempting to postulate that the functions do in fact operate in isolation. Indeed, that assumption has been made, most notably in economic theory. But the assumption is not justified, except in very exceptional circumstances where the participants make a special effort to keep the two functions separate. That may be the case with social scientists who are single-mindedly devoted to the pursuit of knowledge; but it is not true of the participants in the events that social scientists study. For reasons I shall explore later, social scientists, particularly economists, tend to ignore this fact.

When both functions are in operation at the same time they may interfere with each other. For the cognitive function to produce knowledge it must take social phenomena as independently given; only then will the phenomena qualify as facts to which the observer's statements may correspond. Similarly, decisions need to be based on knowledge to produce the desired results. But when both functions operate simultaneously, the phenomena do not consist only of facts but also of intentions and expectations about the future. The past may be uniquely determined, but the future is contingent on the participants' decisions. Consequently the participants cannot base their decisions on knowledge because they have to deal not only with present and past facts but also with contingencies concerning the future. The role that intentions and expectations about the future play in social situations sets up a two-way connection between the participants' thinking and the situation in which they participate, which has a deleterious effect on both: it introduces an element of contingency or uncertainty into the course of events, and it prevents the participants' views from qualifying as knowledge.

For a function to be uniquely determined, it needs an independent variable which determines the value of the dependent variable. In the cognitive function the actual state of affairs is supposed to be the independent variable, and the participants' views the dependent one; in the manipulative function it is the other way round. In reflexive situations each function deprives the other of the independent variable which it would need to produce determinate results. I have given the two-way interference a name: reflexivity. Reflexive situations are characterized by a lack of correspondence between the participants' views and the actual state of affairs. Take the stock market, for example. People buy and sell stocks in anticipation of future stock prices, but those prices are contingent on the investors' expectations. The expectations cannot qualify as knowledge. In the absence of knowledge, participants must introduce an element of judgment or bias into their decision making. As a result, outcomes are liable to diverge from expectations.

Economic theory has gone to great lengths to exclude reflexivity from its subject matter. At first, classical economists simply assumed that market participants base their decisions on perfect knowledge: one of the postulates on which the theory of perfect competition was based was perfect knowledge. Building on those postulates, economists constructed demand curves and supply curves and claimed that those curves governed the participants' decisions. When the construct came under attack, they took refuge behind a methodological convention. Lionel Robbins, who was my professor at the London School of Economics, argued that economics is concerned only with the relationship between demand and supply; what goes into constituting demand and supply is beyond its scope.* By taking demand and supply as independently given he eliminated the possibility that there could be a reflexive interconnection between the two. This approach was later carried to an extreme in rational expectations theory, which somehow contrived to reach the conclusion that future market prices can also be independently determined and are not contingent on the biases and flawed perceptions prevailing among market participants.

I contend that rational expectations theory totally misinterprets how financial markets operate. Although rational expectations theory is no longer taken seriously outside academic circles, the idea that financial markets are self-correcting and tend towards equilibrium remains the prevailing paradigm on which the various synthetic instruments and valuation models which have come to play such a dominant role in financial markets are based. I contend that the prevailing paradigm is false and urgently needs to be replaced.

The fact is that participants cannot base their decisions on knowledge. The two-way, reflexive connection between the cognitive and manipulating functions introduces an element of uncertainty or indeterminacy into both functions. That applies both to market participants and to the financial authorities who are in charge of macro-economic policy and are supposed to supervise and regulate markets. The members of both groups act on the basis of an imperfect understanding of the situation in which they participate. The element of uncertainty inherent in the two-way reflexive

---

*Lionel Robbins, *An Essay on the Nature and Significance of Economic Science* (London: Macmillan, 1932).

connection between the cognitive and manipulative functions cannot be eliminated; but our understanding, and our ability to cope with the situation, would be greatly improved if we recognized this fact.

This brings me to the central idea in my conceptual framework: I contend that social events have a different structure from natural phenomena. In natural phenomena there is a causal chain that links one set of facts directly with the next. In human affairs the course of events is more complicated. Not only facts are involved but also the participants' views and the interplay between them enters into the causal chain. There is a two-way connection between the facts and opinions prevailing at any moment in time: on the one hand participants seek to understand the situation (which includes both facts and opinions); on the other, they seek to influence the situation (which again includes both facts and opinions). The interplay between the cognitive and manipulative functions intrudes into the causal chain so that the chain does not lead directly from one set of facts to the next but reflects and affects the participants' views. Since those views do not correspond to the facts, they introduce an element of uncertainty into the course of events that is absent from natural phenomena. That element of uncertainty affects both the facts and the participants' views. Natural phenomena are not necessarily determined by scientific laws of universal validity. For instance, Heisenberg's uncertainty principle does not determine the behavior of quantum particles or waves, it merely asserts that their behavior cannot be determined. There is a somewhat similar uncertainty principle at work in social events.

I explain the element of uncertainty inherent in social events by relying on the correspondence theory of truth and the concept of reflexivity. Reflexivity has been used in logic to refer to a relation that an object has to itself. I am using it in a somewhat different sense to describe a two-way connection between the participants' thinking and the situation in which they participate.

Knowledge is represented by true statements. A statement is true if and only if it corresponds to the facts. That is what the correspondence theory of truth tells us. To establish correspondence the facts and the statements which refer to them must be independent of each other. It is this requirement that cannot be fulfilled when we are part of the world we seek to understand. That is why participants cannot base their decisions on knowledge. What they lack in knowledge they have to make up for with guesswork based on experience, instinct, emotion, ritual, or other misconceptions. It is the participants' biased views and misconceptions that introduce an element of uncertainty into the course of events.

All this makes eminent sense. The puzzle is why the concept of reflexivity has not been generally recognized. In the case of the financial markets I know the answer: reflexivity prevents economists from producing theories that would explain and predict the behavior of financial markets in the same way that natural scientists can explain and predict natural phenomena. In order to establish and protect the status of economics as a science, economists have gone to great lengths to eliminate reflexivity from their subject matter. I shall argue that, since social events have a different structure from natural phenomena, it was a mistake to model economics on Newtonian physics.

When it comes to other realms of reality, I am on less certain ground because I am less well grounded in philosophy. My impression is that philosophers have grappled with the problem of reflexivity in various ways. Aristotle, for instance, distinguished between theoretical reason (i.e., the cognitive function) and practical reason (i.e., the manipulative function). Being philosophers, however, they were so preoccupied with the cognitive function that they did not give sufficient weight to the manipulative function.

Philosophers recognized and explored the cognitive uncertainty associated with self-referent statements. The problem was first stated by the Cretan philosopher Epimenides when he said that Cretans always lie. The paradox of the liar eventually led Bertrand Russell to distinguish between statements that refer to themselves and those that do not. Analytical philosophers also studied the problems associated with speech acts, statements that make an impact on the situation to which they refer, but their interest was mainly focused on the cognitive aspect of the problem. The fact that social events have a different structure from natural phenomena did not receive proper recognition. On the contrary, Karl Popper, who has been a major source of inspiration for me, declared the doctrine of the unity of method, that is to say, the same methods and criteria ought to apply to the study of natural events and social events. Of course, that is not the only point of view that has been put forward, but it is the prevailing view among social scientists who aspire to the same status as natural scientists. Not all social scientists do so. Anthropologists and most sociologists do not even try to imitate the natural sciences. But they are less influential than those who try.

The theory of reflexivity seeks to illuminate the relationship between thinking and reality. It applies to only a relatively narrow segment of reality. In the realm of natural phenomena, events occur independently of what anybody thinks; therefore, natural science can explain and predict the course of events with reasonable certainty. Reflexivity is confined to social phenomena—more specifically, those situations in which participants cannot base their decisions on knowledge—and it creates difficulties for the social sciences from which the natural sciences are exempt.

Reflexivity can be interpreted as a circularity, or two-way feedback loop, between the participants' views and the actual state of affairs. People base their decisions not on the actual situation that confronts them but on their perception or interpretation of that situation. Their decisions make an impact on the situation (the manipulative function), and changes in the situation are liable to change their perceptions (the cognitive function). The two functions operate concurrently, not sequentially. If the feedback were sequential, it would produce a uniquely determined sequence leading from facts to perceptions to new facts and then new perceptions, and so on. It is the fact that the two processes occur simultaneously that creates an indeterminacy in both the participants' perceptions and the actual course of events. This way of looking at reflexivity will be particularly useful, as we shall see, in understanding the behavior of financial markets. Whether we speak of a circularity, or a feedback mechanism, is a matter of interpretation; but the two-way interaction is real. The circularity is not an error of interpretation; on the contrary, it is the denial of a circularity that is the error. The theory of reflexivity seeks to correct that error.

The difficulties of the social sciences are only pale, second-hand reflections of the predicament in which the participants find themselves. They can affect the course of events—the future is influenced by their decisions—but they cannot base their decisions on knowledge. They are obliged to form a view of the world, but that view cannot possibly correspond to the actual state of affairs. Whether they recognize it or not, they are obliged to act on the basis of beliefs which are not rooted in reality. Misinterpretations of reality and other kinds of misconceptions play a much bigger role in determining the course of events than generally recognized. That is the main new insight that the theory of reflexivity has to offer. The current financial crisis will serve as a persuasive example.

Before expounding the theory in greater detail, I think it may help prepare the ground if I recount how I came to develop it over the years. As the reader will see, the theory grew out of my personal experience. I learned at an early age how ideologies based on false premises can transform reality. I also learned that there are times when the normal rules do not apply, and the abnormal becomes normal.

CHAPTER 2

Autobiography of
a Failed Philosopher

I have always been interested in philosophy. From an early age, I wanted to know who I was, the world into which I was born, the meaning of my life, and, even more, when I became aware of it, the prospect of my death. I started reading classical philosophers early in my teens, but the really important period came during the Nazi occupation of Hungary in 1944 and afterwards, when I emigrated to England in 1947.

The year 1944 was the formative experience of my life. I shall not give a detailed account of it because my father has done it better than I could.* Imagine a child of fourteen, coming from a middle-class background, suddenly confronted with the prospect of being deported and killed just because he is Jewish. Fortunately my father was well prepared for this far-from-equilibrium experience. He had lived through the Russian Revolution in Siberia, and that was the

*Tivadar Soros, *Masquerade: Dancing around Death in Nazi-Occupied Hungary* (New York: Arcade Publishing, 2001).

formative experience of *his* life. Until then he had been an ambitious young man. When World War I broke out, he volunteered to serve in the Austro-Hungarian army. He was captured by the Russians and taken as a prisoner of war to Siberia. Being ambitious, he became the editor of a newspaper produced by the prisoners. The paper was called *The Plank* because handwritten articles were posted on a plank; the authors hid behind the plank and listened to the comments made by the readers. My father became so popular that he was elected the prisoners' representative. When some soldiers escaped from a neighboring camp, their prisoners' representative was shot in retaliation. Instead of waiting for the same thing to happen in his camp, my father organized a group and led the breakout. His plan was to build a raft and sail down to the ocean, but his knowledge of geography was deficient; he did not know that all the rivers in Siberia flow into the Arctic Sea. They drifted for several weeks before they realized that they were heading to the Arctic, and it took them several months to make their way back to civilization across the taiga. In the meantime, the Russian Revolution broke out, and they became caught up in it. Only after a variety of adventures did my father manage to find his way back to Hungary; had he remained in the camp, he would have arrived home much sooner.

My father came home a changed man. His experiences during the Russian Revolution affected him profoundly. He lost his ambition and wanted nothing more from life than to enjoy it. He imparted to his children values that were very different from those of the milieu in which we lived. He had no desire to amass wealth or become socially prominent. On the contrary, he worked only as much as was necessary to make ends meet. I remember being sent to his main client to borrow some money before we went on a ski vacation; my father was grouchy for a few weeks afterwards because he had to work to pay it back. Although we were reasonably prosperous, we were not the typical bourgeois family, and we were proud of being different.

When the Germans occupied Hungary on March 19, 1944, my father knew these were not normal times and the normal rules did not apply. He arranged false identities for his family and a number of others. The clients paid; others received his help for free. Most of them survived. That was his finest hour.

Living with a false identity turned out to be an exhilarating experience for me. We were confronted by mortal danger, and people perished all around us, but we managed not only to survive but to emerge victorious because we were able to help so many others. We were on the side of the angels, and we triumphed against overwhelming odds. I was aware of the dangers, but I did not think they could touch me. It was high adventure, like living through *Raiders of the Lost Ark*. What more could a fourteen-year-old ask for?

After the heady adventures of the Nazi persecution, life started losing its luster during the Soviet occupation. At first, the adventures continued, and we were able to maneuver successfully through perilous situations. The Swiss consulate employed my father to act as the liaison officer with the Russian occupying forces. The Swiss were looking after the Allied interests at the time, so this was a key position. When the Allied Powers established their own representative offices, my father retired because he felt that if he worked for the Allies he would be too exposed. It was a wise decision—he avoided later persecution. But the situation was becoming drab and oppressive for a youth who had become accustomed to adventure. I also thought that it was unhealthy for a young man of fifteen to think exactly like his fifty-year-old father. I told my father that I wanted to get away. "Where would you like to go?" he asked. "To Moscow, to find out about communism, or to London because of the BBC," I replied. "I know the Soviet Union intimately and I can tell you all about it," my father said. That left London. It was not easy to get there, but I arrived in September 1947.

Living in London was a comedown. I had no money and no friends. After my adventurous life, I was full of myself, but the people in London were not interested. I was an outsider looking in, and I discovered loneliness. There was a moment when I ran out of money. I was having a snack at a Lyons Corner House, and after paying for my food I had no money left. "I have touched bottom," I told myself, "and I am bound to rise. This will be a valuable experience." Ever since, I have made sure not to touch bottom again.

I read and thought a lot while working as a swimming pool attendant in Brentford, waiting to be admitted to the London School of Economics (LSE). One of the books I read was Karl Popper's *The Open Society and Its Enemies*. That book struck me with the force of revelation. Popper argued that the Nazi and Communist ideologies have something in common—they both claim to be in possession of the ultimate truth. Since the ultimate truth is beyond human reach, both ideologies had to be based on a biased and distorted interpretation of reality; consequently, they could be imposed on society only by the use of repressive methods. He juxtaposed a different principle of social organization, one that is based on the recognition that the ultimate truth is beyond our reach and that we need institutions that allow people with different views and different interests to live together in peace. He called this principle the open society. Having just lived through the German and Soviet occupations, I became firmly committed to the ideal of an open society.

I also delved deeper into Popper's philosophy. Popper is first and foremost a philosopher of science. He maintained that scientific theories cannot be verified; they have to be treated as hypotheses subject to falsification; as long as they are not falsified, they can be accepted as provisionally true. The asymmetry between verification and falsification provides a solution to the otherwise intractable problem of induction: How can any number of discreet observations be used to verify a theory that claims to be universally valid? Replacing verification with falsification eliminates the need to use inductive logic. I consider this Popper's greatest contribution to the philosophy of science.

I was greatly influenced by Popper's philosophy, but of course I read many other books as well, and I did not accept all of Popper's positions uncritically. In particular, I disagreed with what he called the doctrine of the unity of method—that is to say that the same methods and criteria apply both in the natural and the social sciences. I maintain that there is a fundamental difference between the two, namely that the social sciences deal with events that have thinking participants. These participants base their decisions on their imperfect understanding. Their fallibility creates a difficulty for the understanding of social situations, which is absent in the case of natural phenomena. For that reason the social sciences need to use somewhat different methods and standards from the natural sciences. It may not be possible to draw a hard and fast dividing line between the two—for instance, where does evolutionary psychology or medicine belong? Nevertheless, as I explained in the previous chapter, the difference between natural and social phenomena plays a key role in my view of the world.

My philosophy evolved over the years, but I started forming it already as an undergraduate student at the LSE. I studied economic theory. I was not very good at math, and that led me to question the assumptions on which the mathematical models of economists were based. The theory of perfect competition assumed perfect knowledge, and that assumption was in direct conflict with Popper's contention that our understanding is inherently imperfect. In the course of its development, economic theory was forced to abandon the assumption of perfect knowledge, but it replaced that assumption with others that allowed economic theory to produce universally valid generalizations that were comparable to those of Isaac Newton in physics. The assumptions became increasingly convoluted and gave rise to an imaginary world that reflected only some aspects of reality but not others. That was the world of mathematical models describing a putative market equilibrium. I was more interested in the real world than in mathematical models, and that is what led me to develop the concept of reflexivity.

The theory of reflexivity does not yield determinate results comparable to Newtonian physics; rather, it identifies an element of indeterminacy which is inherent in situations that have participants who operate on the basis of imperfect understanding. Instead of a universal tendency towards equilibrium, financial markets follow a specific one-directional

course. There may be patterns that tend to repeat themselves, but the actual course is indeterminate and unique.
Thus, the theory of reflexivity constitutes a theory of history.
However, the theory emphatically does not qualify as scientific because it does not provide deterministic explanations
and predictions. It is merely a conceptual framework for
understanding events that have human participants. Nevertheless, it served me well later when I became a market participant. Much later, when my success in the financial
markets allowed me to set up a foundation, my theory of history guided me in my philanthropy.

My philosophical explorations did not help me much as a
student. I barely passed my exams. I would have preferred to
stay within the safe walls of academe—I even had a teaching
assistant job prospect at the University of Michigan in Kala-
mazoo, but my grades were not good enough, and I was
forced to go out into the real world. After several false starts, I
ended up working as an arbitrage trader, first in London and
then in New York.* At first I had to forget everything I had
learned as a student in order to hold down my job, but eventually my college education came in very useful. In particular, I
could apply my theory of reflexivity to establish a disequilib-
rium scenario or boom-bust pattern for financial markets.
The rewarding part came when markets entered what I called
far-from-equilibrium territory because that is when the generally accepted equilibrium models broke down. I specialized
in detecting and playing far-from-equilibrium situations with

---

*Arbitrage trading involves exploiting price discrepancies between interrelated
markets. The discrepancies may occur between different locations, like Tokyo
or Johannesburg versus New York, or different securities, like convertible bonds
or warrants versus common stock.

good results. This led to my first published book, *The Alchemy of Finance* (1987), in which I expounded my approach. I called it alchemy to emphasize that my theory does not meet the currently prevailing requirements of scientific method.

To what extent my financial success was due to my philosophy is a moot question because the salient feature of my theory is that it does not yield any firm predictions. Running a hedge fund involves the constant exercise of judgment in a risky environment, and that can be very stressful. I used to suffer from backaches and other psychosomatic ailments, and I received as many useful signals from my backaches as from my theory. Nevertheless, I attributed great importance to my philosophy and particularly my theory of reflexivity. Indeed, I considered it so significant, treasured it so much, that I found it difficult to part with it by putting it in writing and publishing it. No formulation was good enough.

To express my ideas in a few sentences, as I have done here, would have seemed sacrilegious. It had to be a book. As I belabored the points, my arguments became more and more convoluted until I reached a point when I could not understand what I had written the night before. As I have often recounted it, that is when I abandoned my philosophical explorations, returned to the land of the living, and started making money in earnest. But that, too, had its downside. When I resumed my philosophical investigations and published the results in *The Alchemy of Finance*, the philosophical part was dismissed by many critics as the self-indulgence of a successful speculator. That is how I came to consider myself a failed philosopher. Nevertheless, I kept on trying. Once I gave a lecture at the University of Vienna with the title "A Failed Philosopher Tries Again." I found myself in a large hall, looking down on the audience from a cathedra that towered high above the auditorium. I felt inspired by the setting to make an ex cathedra statement, and on the spur of the moment I announced the doctrine of fallibility. It was the best part of my lecture.

Some of the difficulties in formulating my ideas were inherent in the concepts of fallibility and reflexivity; others were self-inflicted. In retrospect, it is clear that I was not precise enough in my formulations and tended to overstate my case. As a result, the professionals whose positions I challenged could dismiss or ignore my arguments on technical grounds without giving them any real consideration. At the same time, some readers could look through my faulty rhetoric and appreciate the ideas that lay behind them. That was particularly true for people engaged in the financial markets, where my demonstrated success led them to look for the reason behind it, and the obscurity of my formulations added to their fascination. My publisher anticipated this and refrained from editing my manuscript. He wanted the book to be the subject of a cult. To this day *The Alchemy of Finance* is read by market participants, taught in business schools, but totally ignored in departments of economics.

Unfortunately, the idea that I was a failed philosopher came to be accepted by those who wrote about me, including my biographer, Michael Kaufman. He quoted my son Robert:

> My father will sit down and give you theories to explain why he does this or that. But I remember seeing it as a kid and thinking, Jesus Christ, at least half of this is bullshit. I mean, you know the reason he changes his position on the market or whatever is because his back starts

killing him. It has nothing to do with reason. He literally goes into a spasm, and it's this early warning sign.

If you're around him a long time, you realize that to a large extent he is driven by temperament. But he is always trying to rationalize what are basically his emotions. And he is living in a constant state of not exactly denial, but rationalization of his emotional state. And it's very funny.*

I harbored grave doubts myself. Although I took my philosophy very seriously, I was not at all certain that what I had to say deserved to be taken seriously by others. I knew that it was significant for me subjectively, but I was uncertain about its objective worth for others. The theory of reflexivity deals with a subject—the relationship between thinking and reality—that philosophers had been discussing for ages. Is it possible to say something new and original about it? After all, both the cognitive function and the participating function can be observed in real life; what can be so original in the concept of reflexivity? It must have been around under some other names. The fact that I am not well versed in the literature made it all the more difficult for me to reach a firm conclusion. Yet I desperately wanted to be taken seriously as a philosopher, and that very ambition turned into my greatest obstacle. I felt obliged to keep on explaining my philosophy because I felt it was not properly understood. All my books followed the same pattern. They recited my theory of history—usually at the end so as not to discourage the readers—

*Quoted in Michael Kaufman, *Soros: The Life and Times of a Messianic Billionaire* (New York: Alfred A. Knopf, 2002), 140.

and applied the theory to the present moment in history. With the passage of time, I overcame my reluctance to part with the concept of reflexivity, and the capsule versions of my philosophy became shorter and, I hope, clearer. In my last book, *The Age of Fallibility*, I put the philosophy up front. I resolved to make it the last presentation, for better or worse, but I was still not sure whether my philosophy deserved to be taken seriously.

Then something happened to change my mind. I was trying to answer the question, how could the propaganda techniques described in Orwell's *1984* be so successful in contemporary America? After all, in *1984* Big Brother was watching you; there was a Ministry of Truth and an apparatus of repression to take care of dissidents. In contemporary America there is freedom of thought and pluralistic media. Yet the Bush administration managed to mislead the people by using Orwellian Newspeak. Suddenly it dawned on me that the concept of reflexivity can shed new light on the question. Until then I had taken it for granted that Orwellian Newspeak could prevail only in a closed society like Orwell's *1984*. In doing so I was slavishly following Karl Popper's argument in favor of the open society, namely, that freedom of thought and expression is liable to lead to a better understanding of reality. His argument hinged on the unspoken assumption that political discourse aims at a better understanding of reality. But the concept of reflexivity asserts that there is such a thing as the manipulative (formerly participating) function, and political discourse can be successfully used to manipulate reality. Why, then, should politicians give preference to the cognitive over the manipulative function? That is appropriate for a social scientist whose aim is the acquisition of knowledge but not for a politician whose primary purpose is to get elected and stay in power.

This insight forced me to reconsider the concept of open society, which I had adopted from Karl Popper rather uncritically. But the insight also did something else. It convinced me that my conceptual framework has an objective value that goes beyond my personal predilection. The concepts of reflexivity and fallibility make an important contribution to our understanding, not because they are something novel or original by themselves but because they can be used to identify and refute widespread and influential misconceptions. One of those misconceptions is what I call the Enlightenment fallacy, which assumes that the purpose of reason is to produce knowledge. I call it a fallacy because it ignores the manipulative function. How deeply rooted the Enlightenment tradition is can be seen from my own experience. By embracing the concept of open society I subscribed to the Enlightenment fallacy even though by developing the concept of reflexivity I was asserting the importance of the manipulative function.

This conclusion removed the doubts I used to entertain about the objective value of my philosophy. Then came the financial crisis which is playing havoc with the financial system and threatens to engulf the economy. It is a vivid demonstration of how much damage misconceptions can cause. The theory of reflexivity offers a genuine alternative to the currently prevailing paradigm. If the theory of reflexivity is valid, the belief that financial markets tend towards equilibrium is false, and vice versa.

I am now ready to submit my conceptual framework to public consideration in the firm conviction that it deserves attention. I am aware of the various shortcomings in my previous presentations, which I hope to have overcome, and I believe that it will be worth the reader's while to make the effort required to understand my philosophy. Needless to say, this makes me very happy. I have been fortunate in making a lot of money and spending it well. But I have always wanted to be a philosopher, and finally I may have become one. What more can one ask for from one life?

CHAPTER 3

The Theory of Reflexivity

Readers may find this chapter somewhat repetitive and hard going. Those who are only interested in the financial markets may skip it or return to it after they have found my interpretation of the current situation convincing. From the author's perspective it remains indispensable—more important than the correct interpretation of the financial crisis. Ideas like radical fallibility, fertile fallacies, the Enlightenment fallacy, and the postmodern fallacy are useful in understanding the current situation and are embedded in my arguments in Part 2.

FALLIBILITY

Having established the significance of my conceptual framework I can now dwell on some of the complexities I swept under the carpet in my summary presentation. I labored on my philosophy over many years. I shall now briefly recount the difficulties I encountered and summarize the conclusions I reached.

I did not make the relationship between fallibility and reflexivity sufficiently clear. People are participants, not just observers, and the knowledge they can acquire is not sufficient to guide them in their actions. They cannot base their decisions on knowledge alone. That is the condition I describe by the word "fallibility." Without fallibility there would be no reflexivity—if people could base their decisions on knowledge the element of uncertainty that characterizes reflexive situations would be removed—but fallibility is not confined to reflexive situations. In other words, fallibility is a more comprehensive condition, and reflexivity is a special case.

People's understanding is inherently imperfect because they are part of reality and a part cannot fully comprehend the whole. In calling our understanding imperfect, I mean that it is incomplete and, in ways that cannot be precisely defined, distorted. The human brain cannot grasp reality directly but only through the information it derives from it. The capacity of the human brain to process information is limited, whereas the amount of information that needs to be processed is practically infinite. The mind is obliged to reduce the available information to manageable proportions by using various techniques—generalizations, similes, metaphors, habits, rituals, and other routines. These techniques distort the underlying information but take on an existence of their own, further complicating reality and the task of understanding it.

Gaining knowledge requires a separation between thoughts and their object—facts must be independent of the statements that refer to them—and that separation is difficult to establish when you are part of what you seek to understand. One must put oneself in the position of a detached observer. The human mind has worked wonders in trying to reach that position, but in the end it cannot fully overcome the fact that it is part of the situation it seeks to comprehend.

Since I started developing my conceptual framework more than fifty years ago, cognitive science has made great progress in explaining how the human brain functions. I should like to invoke a couple of its main tenets because they provide an insight into our fallibility. One is that consciousness is a relatively recent addition to the human brain and has been superimposed on the animal brain, according to George Lakoff. The other is that reason and emotion are inseparable, as noted in the work of Antonio Damasio. These features are reflected in the language we use. Many of the most widely used metaphors have to do with the basic animal functions of vision and locomotion, and they carry an emotional connotation. Up and forward are good, down and backwards are bad; clear and bright are good, muddy and dark are bad. Ordinary language gives a very inexact and emotional view of the world, but it has an uncanny knack for identifying the features that are needed for instant decision making. Logic and mathematics are more precise and objective, but they are of limited use in coping with life. Ideas expressed in ordinary language do not constitute an exact representation of an underlying reality. They compound the complexity of the reality with which people have to cope in the course of their lives.

REFLEXIVITY

I analyzed the relationship between thinking and reality by introducing two functions that connect them in opposite directions. That is how I arrived at the concept of reflexivity.

But in trying to define and explain reflexivity I encountered enormous difficulties. These difficulties continue to haunt me when I discuss reflexivity. I drew a distinction between thinking and reality, whereas what I wanted to say was that thinking is part of reality. I found myself talking about a two-way connection between the course of events and the participants' thinking. That left out a two-way connection between the thinking of the various participants. To take that connection into account I found myself obliged to distinguish between the objective and subjective aspects of reality. The former refers to the course of events, the latter to the participants' thinking. There is only one objective aspect, but there are as many subjective aspects as there are participants. The direct interpersonal relations among participants are more likely to be reflexive than the interaction between perceptions and events because events take longer to unfold.

Once we distinguish between objective and subjective aspects we must also distinguish between reflexive processes and reflexive statements. Reflexive statements belong to the realm of direct interpersonal relations, and those relations are more likely to be reflexive than the course of events.

Consider a statement about the objective aspect: "It is raining." That is either true or false; it is not reflexive. But take a statement like: "You are my enemy." That may be true or false, depending on how you react to it. That is reflexive. Reflexive statements resemble self-referent statements, but the indeterminacy is inherent not in their meaning but in the impact they make. The most famous self-referent statement is the paradox of the liar: "Cretans always lie," said Epimenides. If this statement is true, the Cretan philosopher was not lying, and therefore the statement is false. The ambivalence has nothing to do with the impact of the statement. By contrast, in "You are my enemy" the truth value of the statement depends on your reaction.

In the case of reflexive processes the indeterminacy is introduced by a lack of correspondence between the objective and subjective aspects of a situation. A situation may be reflexive even if the cognitive and manipulative functions operate sequentially and not simultaneously. The process then evolves over a period of time, but it qualifies as reflexive as long as neither the participants' thinking nor the actual state of affairs remains the same at the end of the process as it was at the beginning, and the changes occur as a result of some misconception or misinterpretation by the participants, introducing an element of genuine indeterminacy into the course of events. This renders the situation unpredictable on the basis of scientific laws.

Reflexivity is best demonstrated and studied in the financial markets because financial markets are supposed to be governed by such laws. In other areas the science is less well developed. Even in the financial markets demonstrably reflexive processes occur only intermittently. On a day-by-day basis markets seem to follow certain statistical rules, but occasionally those rules are broken. We may therefore distinguish between humdrum, everyday events that are statistically predictable, and reflexive processes that are not. The latter are of great significance because they alter the course of history. This consideration led me to argue that historic developments are distinguished from everyday events by their reflexivity. But that argument does not stand up. There are many historic events, such as earthquakes, that are not reflexive. The distinction between humdrum and reflexive turned out to be tautological: reflexive developments leave neither the objective nor the subjective aspects of reality unaltered, by definition.

Now that cognitive science and the study of languages have made such progress the concept of reflexivity has been to some extent superseded. Reflexivity distinguishes only two functions: the cognitive and the manipulative. This is a rather crude classification compared to the much more nuanced and detailed analyses of brain and language functions that have become available in recent years. Nevertheless, the concept has not lost its relevance. It pinpoints a distortion in the way philosophers and scientists tend to look at the world. Their primary concern is the cognitive function; insofar as the manipulative function interferes with the proper functioning of cognition, they are inclined to ignore it or to deliberately eliminate it from consideration. Economic theory provides the best example. The theory of perfect competition was built on the assumption of perfect knowledge. When the assumption proved untenable, economists went through ever more elaborate contortions in order to protect the edifice they have erected against the nefarious effects of reflexivity. That is how the assumption of perfect knowledge morphed into the theory of rational expectations—a make-believe world that bears no resemblance to reality. More on that in the next chapter.

THE HUMAN UNCERTAINTY PRINCIPLE

The distinguishing feature of reflexivity is that it introduces an element of uncertainty into the participants' thinking and an element of indeterminacy into the situation in which they participate. Reflexivity bears some resemblance to Werner Heisenberg's uncertainty principle in quantum physics, but there is one important difference: quantum physics deals with phenomena that do not have thinking participants. Heisenberg's discovery of the uncertainty principle did not change the behavior of quantum particles or waves one iota, but the recognition of reflexivity may alter human behavior. Thus, the uncertainty associated with reflexivity affects not only the participants but also the social scientists who seek to establish universally valid laws governing human behavior. This additional element of uncertainty may be described as the human uncertainty principle, and it complicates the task of the social sciences.

THE ENLIGHTENMENT FALLACY

Most of the difficulties I encountered in discussing reflexivity are due to the fact that I had to use a language that does not recognize its existence. I tried to show a two-way interconnection between the participants' thinking and the situation in which they participate, but Western intellectual tradition went out of its way to separate thinking and reality. The effort resulted in dichotomies like those between mind and body, Platonic ideals and observable phenomena, ideas and material conditions, statements and facts. The distinction I have introduced between the subjective and objective aspects of reality falls into the same category.

It is understandable how these dichotomies come into existence: The aim of the cognitive function is to produce knowledge. Knowledge requires statements that correspond to the facts. To establish correspondence, statements and facts have to be treated as separate categories. Hence the pursuit of knowledge leads to the separation of thinking and reality. This dualism had it roots in Greek philosophy, and it came to dominate our view of the world during the Enlightenment.

The philosophers of the Enlightenment put their faith in reason; they saw reality as something separate and independent of reason, and they expected reason to provide a full and accurate picture of reality. Reason was supposed to work like a searchlight, illuminating a reality that lay there, passively awaiting discovery. The possibility that the decisions of thinking agents could influence the situation was left out of account because that would have interfered with the separation between thoughts and their object. In other words, the Enlightenment failed to recognize reflexivity. It postulated an imaginary world where the manipulative function could not interfere with the cognitive function. Indeed, it failed to recognize the manipulative function altogether. It assumed that the sole purpose of thinking was to pursue knowledge. "Cogito ergo sum," said René Descartes. Descartes departed from Aristotle by focusing exclusively on theoretical reason, neglecting what Aristotle called practical reason and I call the manipulative function. This resulted in a distorted view of reality but one that was appropriate to the age when it was formulated.

At the time of the Enlightenment, humankind had relatively little knowledge of or control over the forces of nature, but scientific method held out infinite promise because it was beginning to produce significant results. It was appropriate to think of reality as something out there waiting to be discovered. After all, not even the earth had been fully explored in the eighteenth century. Gathering facts and establishing the relationships among them was richly rewarding. Knowledge was being acquired in so many different ways and from so many different directions that the possibilities seemed unlimited. Reason was sweeping away centuries of superstition and generating in its place a triumphant sense of progress.

The Enlightenment, as it came to be understood, recognized no limit to the acquisition of knowledge. Having identified only a one-way connection between thinking and reality, it treated reality as something independently given that could be fully understood by making statements that corresponded to the facts. This point of view—Popper called it comprehensive rationality—reached its apogee in logical positivism, a philosophy that flourished at the beginning of the twentieth century, primarily in Vienna. Logical positivism held that only empirical statements that could be verified were meaningful, and metaphysical discussions were meaningless.* Logical positivists treated facts and statements as if they belonged to separate universes. The only connection between the two universes was that true statements corresponded to the facts and false statements did not. In these circumstances the facts served as a reliable criterion of truth. This was the foundation of the correspondence theory of truth. The possibility that statements also constituted facts was largely, but not entirely, ignored. A lot of attention was paid to the paradox of the liar.

Bertrand Russell, the British philosopher who was responsible for bringing Ludwig Wittgenstein to Cambridge from Vienna, offered a solution to the paradox of the liar. Russell drew a distinction between two classes of statements: self-referential statements and non-self-referential ones.

---

*Logical positivists made an exception for analytic statements such as "bachelors are unmarried males," which they considered meaningful. This cleared the way to analytical philosophy.

Since the truth value of self-referent statements could not be unequivocally determined, he proposed that they should be excluded from the universe of meaningful statements. This solution might have served to preserve the pristine separation between facts and statements, but it would have prevented people from thinking about issues that concerned them, or even from being conscious of themselves. The absurdity of this position was highlighted by Wittgenstein, who concluded his *Tractatus Logico-Philosophicus* by stating that those who understood the book had to realize that it was meaningless. Shortly thereafter, Wittgenstein abandoned the pursuit of an ideal logical language and replaced it with a study of the workings of ordinary language.

FERTILE FALLACIES

While the Enlightenment's faith in reason was not fully justified, it produced truly impressive results, which were sufficient to sustain the Enlightenment for two centuries. The separation of thinking and reality, for instance, is a fertile fallacy. It is not the only one. Fertile fallacies abound in history. I contend that all cultures are built on fertile fallacies. They are fertile because they flourish and produce positive results before their deficiencies are discovered; they are fallacies because our understanding of reality is inherently imperfect. We are, of course, capable of acquiring knowledge; but if that knowledge proves useful we are liable to overexploit it and extend it to areas where it no longer applies. That is when it becomes a fallacy. That is what happened to the Enlightenment. The ideas of the Enlightenment have become deeply ingrained in our Western civilization, and are difficult to shake. They permeate the writings even of those who are critical of some aspects of the Enlightenment tradition, including myself.

Popper's Scheme of Scientific Method

Karl Popper, a non-card-carrying member of the Vienna Circle, was critical of Wittgenstein and disagreed with comprehensive rationality. He maintained that reason is not capable of establishing the truth of generalizations beyond doubt. Even scientific laws cannot be verified because it is impossible to derive universally valid generalizations from individual observations, however numerous, by deductive logic. Scientific method works best by adopting an attitude of comprehensive skepticism: Scientific laws should be treated as hypotheses which are provisionally valid unless and until they are falsified.

Popper constructed a beautifully simple and elegant scheme of scientific method consisting of three elements and three operations. The three elements are the initial conditions, the final conditions, and the generalizations of universal validity, or scientific laws. The three operations are prediction, explanation, and testing. When the initial conditions are combined with scientific laws they provide a prediction. When the final conditions are combined with those laws they provide an explanation. In this sense, predictions and explanations are symmetrical and reversible.

What is missing from this scheme is the verification of the laws. Here comes Popper's special contribution to our understanding of scientific method. He asserted that scientific laws cannot be verified; they can only be falsified. That is the role of testing. Scientific laws can be tested by pairing off initial conditions with final conditions. If they fail to conform to the scientific law in question, that law has been falsified. Statements that are not subject to falsification do not qualify as scientific. One nonconforming instance may be sufficient to destroy the validity of the generalization, but no amount of conforming instances are sufficient to verify a generalization beyond any doubt. In this sense, there is an asymmetry between verification and falsification. The symmetry between prediction and explanation, the asymmetry between verification and falsification, and the role of testing are the three salient features of Popper's scheme.

Popper's contention that scientific laws cannot be verified resolves the otherwise insoluble problem of induction. Just because the sun has risen in the east every day since man can remember, how can we be sure that it will continue to do so? Popper's scheme removes the need for verification by treating scientific laws as provisionally valid until and unless they have been falsified. Generalizations that cannot be falsified do not qualify as scientific. This interpretation emphasizes the central role that testing plays in scientific method. It establishes a case for critical thinking that allows science to grow, improve, and innovate.

Many features of Popper's scheme have been criticized by professional philosophers. For instance, Popper maintains that the more severe the testing, the greater the value of the generalization that survives it. Professional philosophers question whether the severity of tests and the value of generalizations can be measured. Nevertheless, Popper's assertion makes perfect sense to me, and I can prove it by invoking my experience in the stock market. In the savings and loan crisis of 1986 there were grave doubts whether a mortgage insurance company, Mortgage Guaranty Insurance (nicknamed MAGIC), would be able to survive. The stock fell precipitously, and I bought it in the belief that its business model was sound enough to withstand a severe test. I was right, and I made a killing. Generally speaking, the more an investment thesis is at odds with the generally prevailing view, the greater the financial rewards one can reap if it turns out to be correct. It is on these grounds that I can claim that I accept Popper's scheme more wholeheartedly than the professional philosophers.

Abandoning the Unity of Method

Yet, in spite of his insight that the ultimate truth is beyond the reach of reason, Popper insisted on what he called the doctrine of the unity of scientific method, namely, the same methods and criteria apply to the study of social affairs as to the study of natural phenomena. How could that be? The participants in social affairs act on the basis of fallible understanding. Their fallibility introduces an element of uncertainty into social affairs that does not afflict the study of natural phenomena. The difference needs to be recognized.

I sought to express the difference by introducing the concept of reflexivity. The concept of self-reference had already been extensively analyzed by Russell and others. But self-reference pertains exclusively to the realm of statements. If the separation between the universe of statements and the universe of facts is a distortion of reality, then there has to be a similar effect in the realm of facts. That is the relationship that the concept of reflexivity seeks to express.

To some extent the concept was explored by J. L. Austin and John Searle in their work on speech acts, but I see it in a much wider context. Reflexivity is a two-way feedback mechanism that affects not only statements (by rendering their truth value indeterminate) but also facts (by introducing an element of indeterminacy into the course of events).

Yet, in spite of my preoccupation with the concept of reflexivity, I failed to recognize a flaw in Popper's concept of open society: that political discourse is not necessarily directed at the pursuit of truth. I believe both Popper and I made these mistakes because of *our* preoccupation with the pursuit of truth. Fortunately, these errors are not fatal because the case for critical thinking remains unimpaired and the mistakes can be corrected: we can recognize a difference between the natural and social sciences, and we can introduce the pursuit of truth as a requirement for an open society.

The postmodern attitude towards reality is much more dangerous. While it has stolen a march on the Enlightenment by discovering that reality can be manipulated, it does not recognize the pursuit of truth as a requirement. Consequently, it allows the manipulation of reality to go unhindered. Why is that so dangerous? Because in the absence of proper understanding the results of the manipulation are liable to be radically different from the expectations of the manipulators. One of the most successful instances of manipulation was when President George W. Bush declared a War on Terror and used it to invade Iraq on false pretenses. The outcome was the exact opposite of what he intended: He wanted to demonstrate American supremacy and garner political support in the process; but he caused a precipitous decline in American power and influence and lost political support in the process.

To guard against the dangers of manipulation, the concept of open society originally formulated by Karl Popper needs to be modified in an important respect. What Popper took for granted needs to be introduced as an explicit requirement. Popper assumed that the purpose of critical thinking is to gain a better understanding of reality. That may be true in science but not in politics. The primary purpose of political discourse is to gain power and to stay in power. Those who fail to recognize this are unlikely to *be* in power. The only way in which politicians can be persuaded to pay more respect to reality is by the electorate insisting on it, rewarding those whom it considers truthful and insightful, and punishing those who engage in deliberate deception. In other words, the electorate needs to be more committed to the pursuit of truth than it is at present. Without such a commitment, democratic politics will not produce the desired results. An open society can be only as virtuous as the people living in it.

THE PURSUIT OF TRUTH*

Now that we know reality can be manipulated, it is much more difficult to make a commitment to the pursuit of truth

---

*It is increasingly recognized that the pursuit of truth may not be paramount among scientists, either. The editor of Popper's posthumous works, Mark Notturno, has shocked me by claiming that scientists tend to pursue their institutional self-interests. I have attributed the lack of recognition for my theory of reflexivity to the fact that it demeans the scientific status of economic theory by claiming that the future is genuinely uncertain. This may not be a fruitful line of argument to pursue, however, as indicated by the fact that mainly those who are unsuccessful tend to resort to it. Scientific arguments should be judged on their merits, not on their motives.

than it was at the time of the Enlightenment. For one thing, it is more difficult to establish what the truth is. The Enlightenment regarded reality as something independently given and therefore knowable; but when the course of events is contingent on the biased beliefs and misconceptions of the participants, reality turns into a moving target. For another, it is not at all self-evident why the pursuit of truth should take precedence over the pursuit of power. And even if the electorate were convinced of it, how can the politicians be kept honest?

Reflexivity provides part of the answer, even if it leaves the problem of keeping politicians honest unresolved. It teaches us that the pursuit of truth is important exactly because misconceptions are liable to lead to unintended adverse consequences. Unfortunately the concept of reflexivity is not properly understood. That can be seen from the far-reaching influence that the Enlightenment tradition and, more recently, the postmodern idiom have exerted over people's view of the world. Both interpretations of the relationship between thinking and reality are distorted. The Enlightenment ignores the manipulative function. The postmodern approach goes to the other extreme: By treating reality as a collection of often conflicting narratives, it fails to give sufficient weight to the objective aspect of reality. The concept of reflexivity helps to identify what is missing from each. That said, reflexivity is far from a perfect representation of a very complex reality. The main problem with the concept is that it seeks to describe the relationship between thinking and reality as separate entities when in reality thinking is part of reality.

I have gained a healthy respect for the objective aspect of reality both by having lived under Nazi and Communist regimes and by speculating in the financial markets. *Indeed, I believe that my experience of the far-from-equilibrium conditions of first the German and then the Soviet occupation of Hungary has played an important role in preparing me for a successful career as a hedge fund manager, just as my father's prior experiences during the Russian Revolution helped us to survive the Nazi occupation. And, of course, all these experiences taken together have helped me develop my conceptual framework in which far-from-equilibrium situations like the current financial crisis figure prominently.*

The only experience that teaches you more respect for an external reality that is beyond your control than losing money in the financial markets is death—and death is not an actual experience during one's lifetime. It is much harder for a public that spends much of its time in the virtual reality of television shows, video games, and other forms of entertainment to develop such respect. It is noteworthy that people in America go to great lengths to deny or forget about death. Yet if you disregard reality it is liable to catch up with you. *That is why we should continue to give the cognitive function precedence even after we have become aware that reality can be manipulated and the Enlightenment was built on a distorted worldview.* What better time to bring this argument home than the present, when the unintended adverse consequences of the War on Terror are so clearly visible, and the virtual reality of synthetic financial products has disrupted our financial system? *This is a point I need to pursue a little further even it if takes us further away from the main topic of this book. As I emphasized at the outset, my conceptual framework has implications that reach far beyond the financial markets.*

THE POSTMODERN IDIOM

I had not paid much attention to the postmodern point of view until recently. I did not study it, and I did not fully understand it, but I was willing to dismiss it out of hand because it *was in conflict with my profound respect for an objective reality*. I treated the postmodern view of the world as an overreaction to the Enlightenment's excessive faith in reason, namely, the belief that reason is capable of fully comprehending reality. I did not see any direct connection between the postmodern idiom and totalitarian ideologies and closed societies, although I could see that, by being extremely permissive of different points of view, the postmodern position might encourage the rise of totalitarian ideologies. Recently, I changed my mind. I now see a direct connection between the postmodern idiom and the Bush administration's ideology. That insight came from an October 2004 article by Ron Suskind in the *New York Times Magazine*. This is what he wrote:

> In the summer of 2002 . . . I had a meeting with a senior adviser to Bush. He expressed the White House's displeasure [about a biography of Paul O'Neill, *The Price of Loyalty* by Ron Suskind*], and then he told me something that at the time I didn't fully comprehend—but which I now believe gets to the very heart of the Bush presidency.
>
> The aide said that guys like me were "in what we call the reality-based community," which he defined as people

*Ron Suskind, *The Price of Loyalty: George W. Bush, the White House, and the Education of Paul O'Neill* (New York: Simon & Schuster, 2004).

who "believe that solutions emerge from your judicious study of discernible reality." I nodded and murmured something about enlightenment principles and empiricism. He cut me off. "That's not the way the world really works anymore," he continued. "We're an empire now, and when we act, we create our own reality. And while you're studying that reality—judiciously, as you will—we'll act again, creating other new realities, which you can study too, and that's how things will sort out. We're history's actors . . . and you, all of you, will be left to just study what we do."*

The aide, presumably Karl Rove, did not merely recognize that the truth can be manipulated, he promoted the manipulation of truth as a superior approach. This interferes directly with the pursuit of truth both by declaring it futile and by making the task more difficult through constant manipulation. Moreover, Rove's approach led to the restriction of liberties by using the manipulation of public opinion to enhance the powers and prerogatives of the president. That is what the Bush administration wrought by declaring War on Terror.

I believe the War on Terror provides an excellent illustration of the dangers inherent in Rove's ideology. The Bush administration used the War on Terror to invade Iraq. This was one of the most successful instances of manipulation, yet its consequences for the United States and the Bush administration itself were nothing short of disastrous.

*Ron Suskind, "Without a Doubt," *New York Times Magazine*, October 17, 2004, 51.

The public is now awakening, as if from a bad dream. What can it learn from the experience? That reality is a hard task master, and we manipulate it at our peril: The consequences of our actions are liable to diverge from our expectations. However powerful we are, we cannot impose our will on the world: we need to understand the way the world works. Perfect knowledge is not within our reach; but we must try to come as close to it as we can. Reality is a moving target, yet we need to pursue it. In short, understanding reality ought to take precedence over manipulating it.

As things stand now, the pursuit of power tends to take precedence over the pursuit of truth. Popper and his followers—including me—made a mistake when we took the pursuit of truth for granted. Recognizing the mistake should not lead us to abandon the concept of open society. On the contrary, the experience with the Bush administration ought to reinforce our commitment to open society as a desirable form of social organization. We must alter, however, our definition of what an open society entails. In addition to the familiar attributes of a liberal democracy—free elections, individual liberties, division of powers, the rule of law, etc.— it also entails an electorate that insists on certain standards of honesty and truthfulness. What these standards are need to be first carefully elaborated and then generally accepted.

STANDARDS OF POLITICAL DISCOURSE

Karl Popper, who was first and foremost a philosopher of science, elaborated such standards for scientific discourse and experimentation. To give just one example, laws need to be falsifiable, and experiments need to be replicable to qualify as scientific. The standards of scientific method cannot be applied to politics directly; nevertheless, they serve as an example of the kind of rules that need to be established.

We have identified two crucial differences between science and politics. One is that politics is more concerned with the pursuit of power than the pursuit of truth. The other is that in science there is an independent criterion, namely the facts, by which the truth or validity of statements can be judged. In politics, the facts are often contingent on the participants' decisions. Reflexivity throws a monkey wrench into Popper's model of scientific method.

In *The Alchemy of Finance*, I took issue with Popper's doctrine of the unity of method. I argued that reflexivity prevents the social sciences from meeting the standards of natural science. How could scientific method be expected to produce generalizations which reversibly provide determinate predictions and explanations, when the course of events is inherently indeterminate? We must be content with hunches and alternative scenarios instead of determinate predictions. In retrospect, I probably spent too much time on examining the role of the social scientists and not enough on the participants in social situations. That is why I failed to recognize a flaw in Popper's concept of open society, namely, that politics is more concerned with the pursuit of power than the pursuit of truth. I am now correcting the error by introducing truthfulness and respect for reality as explicit requirements for an open society.

Unfortunately I do not have any clear-cut formula for how that requirement could be met; I can only identify it as an unsolved problem. That is not surprising. The problem is not one that an individual can solve; it requires a change in the attitude of the public.*

I believe political discourse used to abide by much higher standards of truthfulness and respect for the opponents' opinions in the first two hundred years of democracy in America than it does today. I realize that old men usually see the past in rosier colors than the present, but in this case I believe I can justify my claim by invoking the Enlightenment fallacy. As long as people believed in the power of reason they also believed in the pursuit of truth. Now that we have discovered that reality can be manipulated, that belief has been shaken.

This leads to the paradoxical conclusion that the higher standards in politics were based on an illusion, and they were undermined by the discovery of a truth, namely, that reality can be manipulated. This conclusion is reinforced by the fact that Rove was able to write circles around those who still labored under the Enlightenment fallacy and sought to prevail by rational arguments rather than by appealing to the emotions without any regard for the facts. The War on Terror proved to be the most effective slogan of all because it appealed to the strongest of emotions, the fear of death.

To reestablish those higher standards that used to prevail, people must come to realize that reality matters even if it can be manipulated. In other words, people must come to terms with reflexivity. This is no easy task, because a reflexive reality is much more complicated than the reality that the Enlightenment was pursuing. Indeed reality is so complicated

---

*Bernard Williams has a valuable discussion of the point in his book *Truth and Truthfulness: An Essay in Genealogy* (Princeton: Princeton University Press, 2004).

that it can never be fully known. Nevertheless, it remains just as important to gain better understanding as it was at the time of the Enlightenment, and in this respect coming to terms with reflexivity would constitute an important step forward. That was the point I was trying to make in my last book when I said that we need to advance from the Age of Reason to the Age of Fallibility.

RADICAL FALLIBILITY

Fallibility and reflexivity are difficult ideas to accept and to work with. As participants we are constantly called upon to make decisions and to act. But how can we act with any degree of confidence when we may be wrong and our actions may have unintended adverse consequences? It would be much more desirable if we could rely on a doctrine or belief system that lays claim to the ultimate truth. Unfortunately what is desirable is not attainable; the ultimate truth is beyond the reach of the human intellect. Ideologies that promise absolute certainty are bound to be wrong. Only this insight can stop people from adopting such an ideology.

The fact that the ultimate truth is unattainable does not rule out religion. On the contrary, where the ability to obtain knowledge stops, the scope for beliefs opens up. To assert that we cannot base our decisions on knowledge is tantamount to admitting that we cannot avoid relying on beliefs, religious or secular. Indeed, religion has played an important role throughout history. The period since the Enlightenment constitutes an exception. The faith in reason temporarily eclipsed religion. That is how the twentieth century came to be dominated by secular ideologies: socialism, communism, fascism, national socialism, *and I am tempted to add capitalism and market fundamentalism. Now that the distortion in the Enlightenment worldview has become more obvious, religious beliefs have once again come to the fore.*

Science cannot disprove religious or secular ideologies because it is in the nature of such ideologies that they are not subject to falsification. Nevertheless, we are well advised to act on the assumption that we may be wrong. Even if a dogma cannot be proven wrong, our *assertion that the ultimate truth is beyond our reach* cannot be proven right.

So far I am following in Popper's footsteps. I am inclined to go a step further. He asserts that we *may* be wrong. I adopt as my working hypothesis that we are *bound* to be wrong. I call this the postulate of radical fallibility. I base it on the following argument: We are capable of acquiring some insight into reality, but the more we understand, the more there is to be understood. Confronted by this moving target, we are liable to overburden whatever knowledge we have acquired by extending it to areas where it is no longer applicable. In this way, even valid interpretations of reality are bound to give rise to distorted ones. This argument is similar to the Peter Principle, which holds that competent employees are promoted until they reach their level of incompetence.

I find my position buttressed by the findings of cognitive linguistics. George Lakoff, among others, has shown that language employs metaphors rather than strict logic. Metaphors work by transferring observations or attributes from one set of circumstances to another, and it is almost inevitable that the process will be carried too far. This can be best seen in the case of scientific method. Science is a highly successful method for acquiring knowledge. As such, it seems to contradict the postulate of radical fallibility, namely, that we are bound to be wrong. But the process has been carried too far. Because of the success of natural science, social scientists have gone to great lengths to imitate natural science—*and by doing so they reaffirmed the postulate.*

Consider classical economic theory. In its use of the concept of equilibrium, it is imitating Newtonian physics. But in financial markets, where expectations play an important role, the contention that markets tend towards equilibrium does not correspond to reality. Rational expectations theory has gone through great contortions to create an artificial world in which equilibrium prevails, but in that world reality is fitted to the theory rather than the other way round. This is a case to which the postulate of radical fallibility applies.

Even when they failed to meet the rules and standards of scientific method, social thinkers sought to cloak their theories in scientific guise to gain acceptance. Sigmund Freud and Karl Marx both asserted that their theories determined the course of events in their respective fields *because* they were scientific. (At that time, scientific laws were expected to be deterministic.) Popper was successful in unmasking them, particularly Marx, by showing that their theories could not be tested in accordance with his scheme; therefore they were not scientific. But Popper did not go far enough. He did not acknowledge that the study of social phenomena encounters an obstacle that is absent in the natural sciences—reflexivity and the human uncertainty principle. As a consequence, the slavish imitation of natural science does not produce an adequate representation of reality. General equilibrium and rational expectations are far removed from reality. They provide examples of how an approach that produces valid results becomes overexploited and overburdened to the point where it is no longer valid. *That is what the postulate of radical fallibility asserts.*

Suppose my objections to the concepts of general equilibrium and rational expectations were generally upheld, and the theories were abandoned; they would no longer serve as examples of radical fallibility. This shows the fatal flaw in my postulate: It is not necessarily true. Just as Popper did not go far enough, I went too far. We are not bound to be wrong in every situation. Misconceptions can be corrected.

Where does that leave my postulate? It qualifies as a fertile fallacy. It cannot possibly be true because if it were true it would fall into the category of the paradox of the liar. If it were a scientific theory it would be proven false because in Popper's scheme a single instance is sufficient to falsify a theory. But the postulate of radical fallibility is not a scientific theory. It is a working hypothesis and, as such, it works remarkably well. It helps to identify initially self-reinforcing but eventually self-defeating sequences because it presupposes that ideas that work well will be overexploited to the point where they do not work anymore. Indeed, in the course of my investment career I identified many more boom-bust sequences than actually occurred. I discarded most of them by a process of trial and error. The postulate of radical fallibility emphasizes the divergence between reality and the participants' perception of reality, and it focuses attention on misconceptions as a causal factor in history. This leads to a particular interpretation of history that can be illuminating. The present moment is such a time. I regard the War on Terror as a misconception, or false metaphor, that has had a nefarious effect on America and the world. And the current financial crisis can be directly attributed to a false interpretation of how financial markets function.

The postulate of radical fallibility and the idea of fertile fallacies are the hallmarks of my thinking. These concepts sound negative, but they are not. What is imperfect can be improved; radical fallibility leaves infinite room for improvement. In my definition, an open society is an imperfect society that holds itself open to improvement. Open society engenders hope and creativity, although open society is constantly endangered, and history is full of disappointments. In spite of the negative-sounding terminology—imperfect understanding, radical fallibility, fertile fallacies—my outlook on life is profoundly optimistic. That is because from time to time my conceptual framework has allowed me to bring about improvements in real life.

CHAPTER 4

Reflexivity in Financial Markets

So far I have delved into the realm of abstractions. I asserted that there is a two-way connection between thinking and reality which, when it operates simultaneously, introduces an element of uncertainty into the participants' thinking and an element of indeterminacy into the course of events. I called this two-way connection reflexivity, and I asserted that reflexivity distinguishes unique, historical developments from humdrum, everyday events. Now I must provide some concrete evidence that such reflexive developments actually occur and that they are historically significant.

For this purpose, I shall turn first not to political history but to the financial markets. The financial markets offer an excellent laboratory because most of the price and other data are public and quantified. There are plenty of reflexive processes in political and other forms of history as well, but they are more difficult to demonstrate and analyze. The main advantage of financial markets as a laboratory is that my theory of reflexivity is in direct contradiction of a theory that is still widely accepted, namely, the belief that financial markets tend towards equilibrium. If equilibrium theory is correct, reflexivity cannot exist. By the same token, if the theory of reflexivity is correct, equilibrium theory is invalid. The behavior of financial markets needs to be interpreted as a somewhat unpredictable historical process rather than one determined by timelessly valid laws. If that interpretation is accepted for financial markets it can then be extended to other forms of history where reflexivity is less easily observed.

I first published my theory about financial markets in *The Alchemy of Finance*, but the theory of reflexivity did not receive any serious critical consideration. The situation is changing. Economists realize that the prevailing paradigm is inadequate, but they have not yet developed a new one. The subprime mortgage bubble that burst in August 2007 and caused widespread financial dislocations is liable to force the pace. I believe reflexivity as a phenomenon is about to gain much wider recognition, and my theory offers an important insight. The reflexive processes currently unfolding in the financial markets and the global economy constitute an important element in the reality that confronts us at the present moment in history. The danger that they will not be properly understood is very great. That is yet another instance where the cognitive function needs to be given precedence over the manipulative one in order to avoid adverse consequences. I shall summarize my theory in general terms here and apply it to the current situation in Part 2.

EQUILIBRIUM THEORY

Economic theory seeks to imitate the natural sciences. It aims at establishing timelessly valid generalizations that can be used reversibly to explain and predict economic phenomena. In particular the theory of perfect competition modeled itself after Newtonian physics by specifying the equilibrium between supply and demand towards which market prices tend. The theory has been constructed as an axiomatic system like Euclidean geometry: It is based on postulates, and all of its conclusions are derived from them by logical or mathematical calculation. The postulates specify certain ideal conditions, yet the conclusions are supposed to be relevant to the real world. The theory holds that under the specified conditions the unrestrained pursuit of self-interest leads to the optimum allocation of resources. The equilibrium point is reached when each firm produces at a level where its marginal cost equals the market price, and each consumer buys an amount whose marginal utility equals the market price. It can be mathematically calculated that the equilibrium position maximizes the benefit of all participants. It is this line of argument that served as the theoretical underpinning for the *laissez-faire* policies of the nineteenth century, and it is also the basis of the belief in the "magic of the marketplace" that gained widespread acceptance during Ronald Reagan's presidency.

One of the key postulates of the theory as it was originally proposed is perfect knowledge. Other postulates include homogeneous and divisible products and a large enough number of participants so that no individual buyer or seller can influence the market price. The assumption of perfect knowledge was in direct conflict not only with reflexivity but also with the idea of imperfect understanding, convincingly argued by Karl Popper. That is what made me question the theory as a student. Classical economists used the concept of perfect knowledge in exactly that sense in which Popper objected to it. They were laboring under what I now call the Enlightenment fallacy. As the epistemological problems began to surface, exponents of the theory found that they had to use a more modest concept: information. In its modern formulation the theory merely postulates perfect information.*

Unfortunately this assumption is not quite sufficient to support the conclusions of the theory. To make up for the deficiency, modern economists resorted to an ingenious device: they insisted that the demand and supply curves should be taken as independently given. They did not present this as a postulate; rather, they based their claim on methodological grounds. They argued that the task of economics is to study the relationship between supply and demand and not either by itself. Demand may be a suitable subject for psychologists, supply may be the province of engineers or management scientists; both are beyond the scope of economics.† Therefore, both must be taken as given. This was the theory I was taught as a student.

Yet, if we stop to ask what it means that the conditions of supply and demand are independently given, it becomes clear that an additional assumption has been introduced. Otherwise, where would those curves come from? We are dealing with an assumption disguised as a methodological device. Participants are supposed to choose between alternatives in accordance with their scale of preferences. The unspoken

---

*George Stigler, *Theory of Price* (New York: Macmillan, 1966).

†Lionel C. Robbins, *An Essay on the Nature and Significance of Economic Science*, 3d ed. (New York: New York University Press, 1984).

assumption is that the participants *know* what those preferences and alternatives are.

As I shall try to show, this assumption is untenable. The shape of the supply and demand curves cannot be taken as independently given because both of them incorporate the participants' expectations about events that are shaped by their own expectations. Nowhere is the role of expectations more clearly visible than in financial markets. Buy and sell decisions are based on expectations about future prices, and future prices, in turn, are contingent on present buy and sell decisions.

The idea that these decisions can be based on information is quite misleading. The future always involves guesswork. By hook or by crook, economic theory managed to ignore this fact. Economists have recognized and studied asymmetric information but they failed to admit that participants in financial markets cannot base their decisions on information alone. Demand and supply curves are presented in textbooks as though they were grounded in empirical evidence. But there is scant evidence for independently given demand and supply curves. Anyone who trades in markets where prices are continuously changing knows that participants are very much influenced by market developments. Rising prices often attract buyers and vice versa. How could self-reinforcing trends persist if supply and demand curves were independent of market prices? Yet, even a cursory look at commodity, stock, and currency markets confirms that such trends are the rule rather than the exception.

The very idea that events in the marketplace may affect the shape of the demand and supply curves seems incongruous to those who have been reared on classical economics.

The demand and supply curves are supposed to determine the market price. If they were themselves subject to market influences, prices would cease to be uniquely determined. Instead of equilibrium, we would be left with fluctuating prices. This would be a devastating state of affairs. All the conclusions of economic theory would lose their relevance to the real world. It is to prevent this outcome that the methodological device that treats the supply and demand curves as independently given was introduced. Yet there is something insidious about using a methodological device to obscure an assumption that would be untenable if it were spelled out.

Since my student days economists have gone to great lengths to fit the role of expectations into the theory of perfect competition. They developed the theory of rational expectations. I cannot pretend to fully understand the theory because I never studied it. If I understand it correctly, the theory asserts that market participants, in pursuing their self-interest, base their decisions on the assumption that the other participants will do the same. This sounds reasonable, but it is not, because participants act not on the basis of their best interests but on their *perception* of their best interests, and the two are not identical. This has been convincingly demonstrated by experiments in behavioral economics.*
Market participants act on the basis of imperfect understanding, and their actions have unintended consequences. There is a lack of correspondence between expectations and outcomes—between *ex ante* and *ex post*—and it is not rational for

---

*Daniel Kahneman and Amos Tversky, "Prospect Theory: An Analysis of Decision under Risk," *Econometrica* (March 1979): 263–91.

people to act on the assumption that there is no divergence between the two.[†]

Rational expectations theory seeks to overcome this difficulty by claiming that the market as a whole always knows more than any individual participant—sufficiently so that markets manage to be always right. People may get things wrong, and misunderstandings may cause random disturbances; but in the ultimate analysis all market participants use the same model of how the world works, and when they do not, they learn from experience so that in the end they converge on the same model. I have considered this interpretation so far removed from reality that I did not even bother to study it. I have worked with a different model, and the fact that I have been successful using it makes nonsense out of rational expectations, because my performance far exceeds what would be a permissible deviation under the "random walk" theory.

A Contradictory Theory

I contend that financial markets are always wrong in the sense that they operate with a prevailing bias, but in the normal course of events they tend to correct their own excesses. Occasionally the prevailing bias can actually validate itself by influencing not only market prices but also the so-called fundamentals that market prices are supposed to reflect.

[†]Roman Frydman and Michael D. Goldberg, *Imperfect Knowledge Economics: Exchange Rates and Risk* (Princeton: Princeton University Press, 2007); Roman Frydman and Edmund Phelps, *Individual Forecasting and Aggregate Outcomes: Rational Expectations Examined* (Cambridge: Cambridge University Press, 1983).

That is the point that people steeped in the prevailing paradigm have such difficulty grasping. Many critics of reflexivity claimed that I was merely belaboring the obvious, namely that the participants' biased perceptions influence market prices. But the crux of the theory of reflexivity is not so obvious; it asserts that market prices can influence the fundamentals. The illusion that markets manage to be always right is caused by their ability to affect the fundamentals that they are supposed to reflect. The change in the fundamentals may then reinforce the biased expectations in an initially self-reinforcing but eventually self-defeating process. Of course such boom-bust sequences do not occur all the time. More often the prevailing bias corrects itself before it can affect the fundamentals. But the fact that they can occur invalidates the theory of rational expectations. When they occur, boom-bust processes can take on historic significance. That is what happened in the Great Depression, and that is what is unfolding now, although it is taking a very different shape.

In *The Alchemy of Finance* I cite many examples of boom-bust processes or bubbles from the financial markets. Each case involves a two-way, reflexive connection between market valuations and the so-called fundamentals that sets up some kind of short circuit between them whereby valuations affect the fundamentals that they are supposed to reflect. The short circuit may take the form of equity leveraging, that is, the issue of additional shares at inflated prices, but more commonly it involves the leveraging of debt. Most but not all cases involve real estate, commercial or residential, where the willingness to lend influences the value of the collateral. In the international banking crisis of the 1980s the short circuit occurred in sovereign borrowing; no collateral was involved, but the banks' willingness to lend affected the so-called debt ratios which determined the countries' ability to borrow.

THE CONGLOMERATE BOOM
OF THE 1960S

One of my early successes as a hedge fund manager was in exploiting the conglomerate boom that unfolded in the late 1960s. It started when the managements of some high-technology companies specializing in defense recognized that the prevailing growth rate their companies enjoyed could not be sustained in the aftermath of the Vietnam War. Companies such as Textron, LTV, and Teledyne started to use their relatively high-priced stock to acquire more mundane companies, and, as their per-share earnings growth accelerated, their price-earnings multiples, instead of contracting, expanded. They were the path breakers. The success of these companies attracted imitators; later on, even the most humdrum company could attain a higher multiple simply by going on an acquisition spree. Eventually, a company could achieve a higher multiple just by promising to put it to good use by making acquisitions.

Managements developed special accounting techniques that enhanced the beneficial impact of acquisitions. They also introduced changes in the acquired companies: They streamlined operations, disposed of assets, and generally focused on the bottom line, but these changes were less significant than the impact on per-share earnings of the acquisitions themselves.

Investors responded like pigs at the trough. At first, the record of each company was judged on its own merit, but gradually conglomerates became recognized as a group. A new breed of investors emerged: the early hedge fund managers, or gunslingers. They developed direct lines of communication with the managements of conglomerates, and conglomerates placed so-called letter stock directly with fund managers. The placement price was at a discount to the market price, but the stock could not be resold for a fixed period. Gradually, conglomerates learned to manage their stock prices as well as their earnings.

The misconception on which the conglomerate boom rested was the belief that companies should be valued according to the growth of their reported per-share earnings no matter how the growth was achieved. The misconception was exploited by managers who used their overvalued stock to buy companies on advantageous terms, thereby inflating the value of their stock even further. Analytically, the misconception could not have arisen if investors had understood reflexivity and realized that equity leveraging, that is, selling stock at inflated valuations, can generate earnings growth.

Multiples expanded, and eventually reality could not sustain expectations. More and more people became aware of the misconception on which the boom rested even as they continued to play the game. To maintain the momentum of earnings growth, acquisitions had to be larger and larger, and eventually conglomerates ran into the limits of size. The turning point came when Saul Steinberg of the Reliance Group sought to acquire Chemical Bank: It was fought and defeated by the white shoe establishment of the time.

When stock prices started to fall, the decline fed on itself. As the overvaluation diminished, it became impractical to make new acquisitions. The internal problems that had been swept under the carpet during the period of rapid external growth began to surface. Earnings reports revealed unpleasant surprises. Investors became disillusioned, and conglomerate managements went through their own crises: After the heady days of success, few were willing to buckle down to the drudgery of day-to-day management. As the president of one corporation told me: "I have no audience to play to." The situation was aggravated by a recession, and many of the high-flying conglomerates literally disintegrated. Investors were prepared to believe the worst, and for some companies the worst occurred. For others, reality turned out to be better than expectations, and eventually the situation stabilized. The surviving companies, often under new management, slowly worked themselves out from under the debris.

Real Estate Investment Trusts

My best-documented encounter with a boom-bust sequence was that with real estate investment trusts, or REITs. REITs are a special corporate form brought into existence by legislation. Their key feature is that if they disburse more than 95 percent of their income, they can distribute it free of corporate taxation. The opportunity created by this legislation remained largely unexploited until 1969, when numerous mortgage trusts were founded. I was present at the creation, and, fresh from my experience with conglomerates, I recognized their boom-bust potential. I published a research report, where I argued that the conventional method of security analysis does not apply. Analysts try to predict the future course of earnings and then to estimate the price that investors may be willing to pay for those earnings. This method is inappropriate to mortgage trusts because the price that investors are willing to pay for the shares is an important factor in determining the future course of earnings. Instead of predicting future earnings and valuations separately, we should try to predict the future course of the entire initially self-reinforcing but eventually self-defeating process.

I then sketched out a drama in four acts. It starts with an overvaluation of the early mortgage trusts that allows them to justify the overvaluation by issuing additional shares at inflated prices; then come the imitators, who destroy the opportunity. The scenario ends in widespread bankruptcies.

My report had an interesting history. It came at a time when hedge fund managers had suffered severe losses in the collapse of the conglomerates. Since they were entitled to a share in the profits but they did not have to share in the losses, they were inclined to grasp at anything that held out the prospect of quickly recouping their losses. They instinctively understood how a reflexive process works because they had just participated in one, and they were eager to play again. The report found a tremendous response, the extent of which I realized only when I received a telephone call from a bank in Cleveland asking for a fresh copy of my report because theirs had gone through so many Xerox machines that it was no longer legible. There were only a few mortgage trusts in existence at the time, but the shares were so eagerly sought after that they nearly doubled in price in the space of a month or so. Demand generated supply, and a host of new issues came to market. When it became clear that the supply of new mortgage trusts was inexhaustible, prices fell almost as rapidly as they had risen. Obviously the readers of my report had failed to take into account the ease of entry, and their mistake was corrected in short order. Nevertheless, their initial enthusiasm helped to get the self-reinforcing process described in the report under way. Subsequent events took the course outlined in the report. Mortgage trusts enjoyed a boom that was not as violent as the one that came after the publication of my report, but it turned out to be more enduring.

I had invested heavily in mortgage trusts at the time I wrote my report and took some profits when the reception of my study exceeded my expectations. But I was sufficiently carried away by my own success to be caught holding an inventory of shares when the downdraft came. I hung on, and I even increased my positions. I continued to follow the industry closely for a year or so and eventually sold my holdings, realizing good profits. Then I lost touch with the group until a few years later when the problems began to surface. When I became aware of them I was tempted to establish short positions, but I was handicapped because I was no longer familiar with the companies. Nevertheless, when I reread the report I had written several years earlier, I found it so convincing that I decided to sell the group short more or less indiscriminately. Moreover as the shares fell I maintained the same level of exposure by selling additional shares short. My original prediction was fulfilled, and most mortgage trusts went broke. The result was that I reaped more than 100 percent profit on my short positions—a seeming impossibility since the maximum profit on a short position is 100 percent. (The explanation is that I kept on selling additional shares.)

THE INTERNATIONAL BANKING CRISIS
OF THE 1980s

All boom-bust processes contain an element of misunderstanding or misconception. In the two cases I have described, the process took the form of equity leveraging, that is, issuing shares at inflated prices, which was made possible by a misconception about earnings growth: Growth achieved by issuing additional shares at inflated prices was accorded the same premium as growth achieved by other means. Boom-bust processes, or bubbles, are more commonly associated with leveraging of debt rather than equity leveraging, but I analyzed only one instance in *The Alchemy of Finance*: the international banking crisis of the 1980s, which arose out of excessive lending to developing countries in the 1970s.

After the oil shock of 1973, caused by the formation of OPEC (Organization of the Petroleum Exporting Countries), the large money center banks were flooded with deposits from the oil producing countries, and they rechanneled them mainly to oil-importing countries that had to finance their balance of payments deficits. Banks used so-called debt ratios to evaluate the creditworthiness of the borrowing countries, but they failed to realize that the debt ratios were affected by their own lending activities, until it was too late.

In cases of debt leveraging the misconception consists of a failure to recognize a reflexive, two-way connection between the creditworthiness of the borrowers and the willingness of the creditors to lend: Usually there is collateral involved, and the most common form of collateral is real estate. Bubbles arise when banks treat the value of the real estate as if it were independent of the banks' willingness to lend against it. The international banking crisis of the 1980s was somewhat different. The debtors were sovereign countries, and they pledged no collateral. Their creditworthiness was measured by the debt ratios, which turned out to be reflexive: Instead of being independently given, the debt ratios of borrowing countries were inflated during the 1970s by the banks' willingness to lend to them and an associated boom in commodity prices. The first country to run into severe difficulties was Mexico, which was an oil producing country. (Hungary preceded it but the problem was contained.) Since the international banking crisis of the 1980s I have witnessed several real estate bubbles in Japan, Britain, and the United States. The misconception can manifest itself in different guises, but the principle is always the same. What is amazing is that it keeps recurring.

THE BOOM-BUST MODEL

Using the conglomerate boom as my model, I devised a typical boom-bust sequence. The drama unfolds in eight stages. It starts with a prevailing bias and a prevailing trend. In the case of the conglomerate boom, the prevailing bias was a preference for rapid earnings growth per share without much attention to how it was brought about; the prevailing trend was the ability of companies to generate high earnings growth per share by using their stock to acquire other companies selling at a lower multiple of earnings. In the initial stage (1) the trend is not yet recognized. Then comes the period of acceleration (2), when the trend is recognized and reinforced by the prevailing bias. That is when the process approaches far-from-equilibrium territory. A period of testing (3) may intervene when prices suffer a setback. If the bias and trend survive the testing, both emerge stronger than ever, and far-from-equilibrium conditions, in which the normal rules no longer apply, become firmly established (4). *If the bias and trend fail to survive the testing, no bubble ensues.* Eventually there comes a moment of truth (5), when reality can no longer sustain the exaggerated expectations, followed by a twilight period (6), when people continue to play the game although they no longer believe in it. Eventually a crossover or tipping point (7) is reached, when the trend turns down and the bias is reversed, which leads to a catastrophic downward acceleration (8), commonly known as the crash.

The boom-bust model I devised has a peculiarly asymmetric shape. It tends to start slowly, accelerate gradually and then fall steeper than it has risen. I have selected some

THEORY

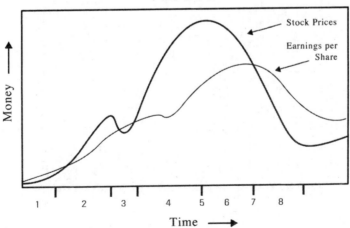

real-life examples that resemble the prototype—although one of the graphs I am using here, LTV, is a little too symmetrical to serve as a good illustration.

(Courtesy of Securities Research Company, a Division of Babson-United Investment Advisors, Inc., 208 Newbury St., Boston, MA 02116.)

OGDEN CORP. [OG]

(Courtesy of Securities Research Company, a Division of Babson-United Investment Advisors, Inc., 208 Newbury St., Boston, MA 02116.)

Exactly the same sequence could be observed in the international banking crisis. It followed the same asymmetric pattern—slow start, gradual acceleration in the boom phase, a moment of truth followed by a twilight period, and a catastrophic collapse. The reason I did not use it as my paradigm was that it did not lend itself to a graphic presentation. In the conglomerate boom, I could draw a chart showing stock

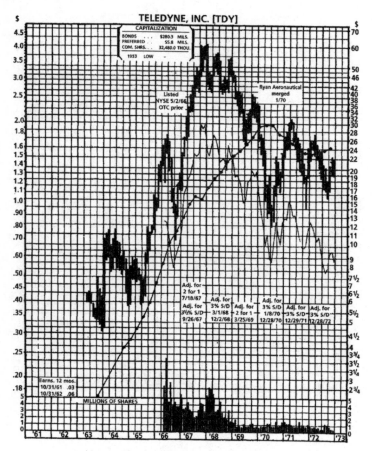

(Courtesy of Securities Research Company, a Division of Babson-United Investment Advisors, Inc., 208 Newbury St., Boston, MA 02116.)

prices and earnings per share; in the international banking crisis I could not create a similar graph *because I could not find an equivalent for earnings per share.*

OTHER FORMS OF REFLEXIVITY

It would be a mistake to think, however, that reflexive processes always manifest themselves in the form of a bubble. They can take many other forms. In freely floating exchange rate regimes, for instance, the reflexive relationship between market valuations and the so-called fundamentals tends to generate large multi-year waves. There is no difference between up and down, except in the case of runaway inflation, and there is no sign of the asymmetry that characterizes bubbles; there is even less evidence of a tendency towards equilibrium.

It is important to realize that two-way, reflexive connections are much more common in financial markets than boom-bust sequences. Market participants act on the basis of imperfect understanding at all times. Consequently market prices usually express a prevailing bias rather than the correct valuation. In the majority of cases, the valuations are proven wrong by subsequent evidence, and the bias is corrected, only to be replaced by a different bias. Only once in a blue moon does a prevailing bias set in motion an initially self-reinforcing but eventually self-defeating process. It happens only when the prevailing bias finds some kind of short circuit that allows it to affect the fundamentals. This is usually associated with some form of leveraged debt or equity. Both market prices and economic conditions may then move far beyond anything that would be possible in the absence of a short circuit, and the correction, when it comes, may have catastrophic consequences.

Markets versus Regulators

Because financial markets do not tend towards equilibrium they cannot be left to their own devices. Periodic crises bring forth regulatory reforms. That is how central banking and the regulation of financial markets have evolved. While boom-bust sequences occur only intermittently, the reflexive interplay between financial markets and the financial authorities is an ongoing process. The important thing to realize is that both market participants and financial authorities act on the basis of imperfect understanding; that is what makes the interaction between them reflexive.

Misunderstandings by either side usually stay within reasonable bounds because market prices provide useful information which allows both sides to recognize and correct their mistakes, but occasionally mistakes prove to be self-validating, setting in motion vicious or virtuous circles. Such circles resemble boom-bust processes in the sense that they are initially self-reinforcing but eventually self-defeating. Vicious and virtuous circles are few and far between, while reflexive interactions go on all the time. Reflexivity is a universal condition, while bubbles constitute a special case.

The distinguishing feature of reflexive processes is that they contain an element of uncertainty or indeterminacy. That uncertainty ensures that the behavior of financial markets is not determined by universally valid generalizations but follows a unique, irreversible path. Within that one-directional process we may distinguish between humdrum, everyday events, which are repetitive and lend themselves pretty well to statistical generalizations, and unique, historical events whose outcome is genuinely uncertain. Bubbles and other vicious or virtuous circles belong to the latter category. It should be realized, however, that reflexive, circular relationships do not necessarily generate historically significant processes. Those which are self-defeating to start with disappear without trace. Others are aborted along the way. Relatively few reach far-from-equilibrium territory. Moreover no process takes place in total isolation. Usually there are several reflexive processes going on at the same time, interfering with each other and producing irregular shapes. Regular patterns arise only on those rare occasions when a particular process is so powerful that it overshadows all the others. Perhaps I did not make this point sufficiently clear in *The Alchemy of Finance*.

THE FLAW IN EQUILIBRIUM THEORY

Equilibrium theory is not without merit. It provides a model with which reality can be compared. When I speak of far-from-equilibrium conditions I am also using the concept of equilibrium.* And economists have made many valiant attempts to adjust their models to take account of reality. So-called second-generation business cycle models have sought to analyze boom-bust situations. I cannot judge their validity,

---

*This could be easily misunderstood. Indeed it was misunderstood by one of my correspondents; hence this footnote. When I speak of far-from-equilibrium conditions, I am using "equilibrium" as a figure of speech. I do not mean to imply that there is a stable equilibrium from which a boom-bust process occasionally deviates. I think of equilibrium as a moving target because market prices can affect the fundamentals they are supposed to reflect.

but they certainly lack the simplicity of my boom-bust model. They remind me of pre-Copernican astronomers who sought to adjust their paradigm, which was circular, to the path followed by the planets, which is elliptical.

It is time for a new paradigm, and one is readily available in the theory of reflexivity—I mean the general theory, not just the boom-bust model. The theory cannot hope to gain scientific acceptance, however, without a fundamental reconsideration of what is to be expected from a theory dealing with social phenomena. If it has to meet the standards and criteria that apply to theories of natural science, the theory of reflexivity cannot possibly qualify because the theory asserts that there is a fundamental difference between the structure of natural and social events. If reflexivity introduces an element of indeterminacy into social events, then those events cannot possibly be predicted in a determinate fashion.

The prevailing paradigm asserts that financial markets tend towards equilibrium. That has led to the notion that actual prices deviate from a theoretical equilibrium in a random manner. While it is possible to construct theoretical models along those lines, the claim that those models apply to the real world is both false and misleading. It leaves out of account the possibility that the deviations may be self-reinforcing in the sense that they may alter the theoretical equilibrium. When that happens, risk calculations and trading techniques based on these models are liable to break down. In 1998 Long-Term Capital Management, a highly leveraged hedge fund employing such trading techniques and advised by two economists who got the Nobel Prize for devising the models, ran into trouble and had to be rescued with the help of the New York Federal Reserve. The techniques and models were modified, but the basic approach was not abandoned. It was observed that price deviations did not follow the normal shape of a bell curve, but had a thick tail. To allow for the extra risk posed by this phenomenon, stress tests were introduced to supplement value-at-risk calculations. But the reason for the thick tails was left unexplained. The reason is to be found in self-reinforcing price movements; but reflexivity continued to be ignored, and the use of mistaken models—particularly in the design of synthetic financial instruments—continued to spread. This is at the root of the current financial crisis, which will be discussed in Part 2.

Renouncing the Unity of Method

The belief that markets tend towards equilibrium has given rise to policies which seek to give financial markets free rein. I call these policies market fundamentalism, and I contend that market fundamentalism is no better than Marxist dogma. Both ideologies cloak themselves in scientific guise in order to make themselves more acceptable, but the theories they invoke do not stand up to the test of reality. They use scientific method to manipulate reality, not to understand it. The fact that scientific method can be used in such a way should be a warning sign that there is something wrong with applying the same methods and criteria to both natural and social science. As I have shown in my discussion of the human uncertainty principle, social situations can be influenced by making statements about them. In other words, they can be manipulated. One of Karl Popper's contributions was to show that ideologies like Marxism do not qualify as scientific. But he did not go far enough. He did not recognize that mainstream economics can also be exploited in the same nonscientific way. The fault lies with the doctrine of the unity of method. By endowing social science with the prestige of natural science it allows scientific theories to be used for manipulative rather than cognitive purposes.

The trap can be avoided, however. All we have to do is renounce the doctrine and adopt the theory of reflexivity. There is a heavy price to pay: Economists have to accept a reduction in their status. No wonder that they put up resistance. But if the objective is to pursue the cognitive function, the price is well worth paying. Not only does the theory of reflexivity provide a better explanation of how financial markets function, but it is also less conducive to the manipulation of reality than the currently prevailing scientific theories because it avoids making excessive claims about its ability to predict and explain social phenomena. Once we recognize that reality can be manipulated, our first priority ought to be to prevent the manipulative function from interfering with the pursuit of knowledge. The theory of reflexivity serves that purpose well by proclaiming that social events become unpredictable whenever reflexivity makes its presence felt. Accordingly we must reduce our expectations for the social sciences. We cannot expect reflexive events to be determined according to timelessly valid generalizations when reflexivity contains an element of uncertainty and indeterminacy (uncertainty relates to the participants' thinking, indeterminacy to the course of events).

One possible objection to abandoning the doctrine of the unity of method is that it is impossible to draw a hard and fast dividing line between the natural and social sciences. But if we follow this line of argument we need not be bothered by the fact that the dividing line between the natural and social sciences is a fuzzy one. Whenever reflexivity rears its ugly head we must reduce our expectations about predictability.

The New Paradigm

Let me spell out how the new paradigm differs from the old one. By applying the postulate of radical fallibility to financial markets, one can assert that, instead of being always right, financial markets are always wrong. Markets have the ability, however, both to correct themselves and occasionally to make their mistakes come true by a reflexive process of self-validation. That is how they can appear to be always right. To be specific, financial markets cannot predict economic downturns accurately, but they can cause them.

Participants act on the basis of imperfect understanding. They base their decisions on incomplete, biased, and misconceived interpretations of reality, not on knowledge, and the outcomes are liable to diverge from expectations. The divergence provides useful feedback on the basis of which they can adjust their behavior. Such a process is unlikely to produce satisfactory results all the time. Indeed markets move away from a theoretical equilibrium almost as often as they move towards it, and they can get caught up in initially self-reinforcing but eventually self-defeating processes. Bubbles often lead to financial crises. Crises, in turn, lead to the regulation of financial markets. That is how the financial system has evolved—periodic crises leading to regulatory reforms.

That is why financial markets are best interpreted as a historical process, and that is why that process cannot be understood without taking into account the role of the regulators. In the absence of regulatory authorities, financial markets would be bound to break down, but in reality breakdowns rarely occur because markets operate under constant supervision, and even if the authorities tend to be sluggish in normal times, they become alert in an emergency—at least in democracies.

Most of the reflexive processes involve an interplay between market participants and regulators. To understand that interplay it is important to remember that the regulators are just as fallible as the participants. Changes in the regulatory environment place every crisis into a unique historical context. That alone is sufficient to justify my claim that the behavior of markets is best regarded as a historical process.

Market fundamentalists blame market failures on the fallibility of the regulators, and they are half right: Both markets and regulators are fallible. Where market fundamentalists are totally wrong is in claiming that regulations ought to be abolished on account of their fallibility. That happens to be the inverse of the Communist claim that markets ought to be abolished on account of their fallibility. Karl Popper (and Friedrich Hayek) have demonstrated the dangers of the Communist ideology. It will advance our understanding of reality if we recognize the ideological character of market fundamentalism. The fact that regulators are fallible does not prove that markets are perfect. It merely justifies reexamining and improving the regulatory environment.

When do the reflexive connections which are endemic in financial markets turn into self-reinforcing, historically significant processes which affect not only prices in the financial markets but also the so-called fundamentals that those prices are supposed to reflect? That is the question that a theory of reflexivity has to answer if it is to be of any value. The subject deserves more detailed investigation, but based on theoretical arguments and empirical evidence, my preliminary hypothesis is that there has to be both some form of credit or leverage and some kind of misconception or misinterpretation involved for a boom-bust process to develop. That is the hypothesis I am now submitting for testing. As I said before, the main insight my conceptual framework has to offer is that misconceptions play a significant role in the making of history. This message is particularly relevant to understanding what is happening in the financial markets at the present moment in history.

One of the major differences between the new paradigm and the old one is that the new one takes a more cautionary approach to the use of leverage. The theory of reflexivity recognizes the uncertainties associated with the fallibility of both regulators and market participants. The prevailing paradigm acknowledges only known risks and fails to allow for the consequences of its own deficiencies and misconceptions. That lies at the root of the current turmoil.

PART **II**

The Current Crisis
and Beyond

CHAPTER 5

The Super-Bubble Hypothesis

We are in the midst of a financial crisis the likes of which has not been seen since the Great Depression of the 1930s. To be sure, it is not the prelude to another Great Depression. History does not repeat itself. The banking system will not be allowed to collapse as it did in 1932 exactly because its collapse then caused the Great Depression. At the same time, the current crisis is not comparable to the periodic crises which have afflicted particular segments of the financial system since the 1980s—the international banking crisis of 1982, the savings and loan crisis of 1986, the portfolio insurance debacle of 1987, the failure of Kidder Peabody in 1994, the emerging market crisis of 1997, the failure of Long Term Capital Management in 1998, the technology bubble of 2000. This crisis is not confined to a particular firm or a particular segment of the financial system; it has brought the entire system to the brink of a breakdown, and it is being contained only with the greatest difficulty. This will have far-reaching consequences. It is not business as usual but the end of an era.

To explain what I mean by this somewhat bombastic statement, I shall have recourse to the theory of reflexivity and the boom-bust model I introduced in chapter 4, but the explanation I shall provide will be far from simple. There is not just one boom-bust process or bubble to consider but two: the housing bubble and what I shall call a longer-term super-bubble. The housing bubble is quite straightforward; the super-bubble is much more complicated. To further complicate matters the two bubbles did not develop in isolation; they are deeply imbedded in the history of the period. In particular, the super-bubble cannot be understood without taking into account the asymmetric character of the international financial system; the recent economic strength of China, India, and some oil- and raw material-producing countries; the commodities boom; an exchange rate system that is partly floating, partly tied to the dollar, and partly in between; and the increasing unwillingness of the rest of the world to hold dollars.

The U.S. Housing Bubble

In the aftermath of the technology bubble that burst in 2000 and the terrorist attack of September 11, 2001, the Federal Reserve lowered the federal funds rate to 1 percent and kept it there until June 2004. This allowed a housing bubble to develop in the United States. Similar bubbles could be observed in other parts of the world, notably the United Kingdom, Spain, and Australia. What sets the United States housing bubble apart from the others is its size and importance for the global economy and the international financial system. The housing market turned down earlier in Spain than in the United States, but that passed unnoticed, except locally. By contrast, U.S. mortgage securities have been widely distributed all over the world with some European, particularly German, institutional holders even more heavily involved than American ones.

Taken on its own the United States housing bubble faithfully followed the course prescribed for it by my boom-bust model. There was a prevailing trend—ever more aggressive relaxation of lending standards and expansion of loan-to-value ratios—and it was supported by a prevailing misconception that the value of the collateral was not affected by the willingness to lend. That is the most common misconception that has fueled bubbles in the past, particularly in the real estate area. What is amazing is that the lesson has still not been learned.

The growth of the bubble can be vividly illustrated by a few charts. In Chart 1, the declining line shows the savings rate (right scale), the rising one, house prices adjusted for inflation. Chart 2 shows the unprecedented increase in mortgage debt. Americans have added more household mortgage debt in the last six years than in the prior life of the mortgage market. Chart 3 shows the decline in credit quality. Since the rating agencies based their valuations on past loss experience, and loss experience improved during rising house prices, the rating agencies became increasingly generous in the valuations of collateralized mortgage obligations. At the same time, mortgage originators became increasingly aggressive in their residential lending practices (which is not picked up in this chart). Towards the end, houses could be bought with no money down, no questions asked. The 2005 and 2006 vintage subprime and Alt-A mortgages are of notoriously low quality. Chart 4 shows the growing share of subprime and Alt-A originations. In 2006, 33 percent of all mortgage originations fell into these two categories. Charts 3 and 4 together indicate the deterioration in credit quality. The process was driven by the pursuit of fee income. Chart 5 shows the rise of Moody's revenues from the rating of structured products. By 2006, Moody's revenues from structured products were on par with revenues from its traditional bond rating business. Chart 6 shows the exponential growth of synthetic products.

The bubble started slowly, lasted for several years, and did not reverse itself immediately when interest rates started rising, because it was sustained by speculative demand, aided and abetted by ever more aggressive lending practices and ever more sophisticated ways of securitizing mortgages. Eventually the moment of truth arrived in the spring of 2007, when the subprime problem pushed New Century Financial Corporation into bankruptcy, which was followed by a twilight period when housing prices were falling but people failed to realize that the game was over. The chief executive officer of Citibank, Chuck Prince, was reported saying that "When the music stops, in terms of liquidity, things will be complicated. But as long as the music is playing, you've got to get up and dance. We're still dancing."* When the tipping point was finally reached, in August 2007, there was a catastrophic acceleration on the downside aggravated by a contagion that spread from one segment of the market to another. That was reminiscent of the wrecking ball that knocked down one country after another in the emerging market cri-

---

*Michiyo Nakamoto and David Wighton, "Bullish Citigroup Is 'Still Dancing' to the Beat of the Buy-Out Boom," *Financial Times*, July 10, 2007.

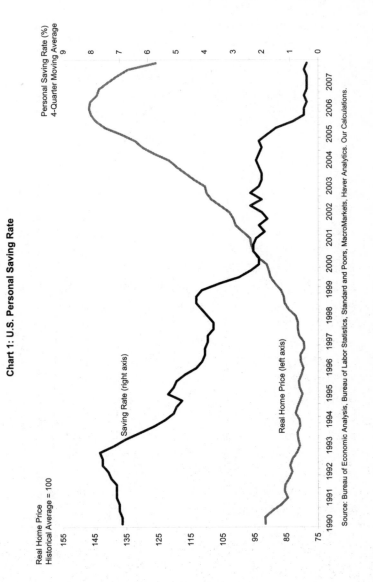

Chart 1: U.S. Personal Saving Rate

Source: Bureau of Economic Analysis, Bureau of Labor Statistics, Standard and Poors, MacroMarkets, Haver Analytics. Our Calculations.

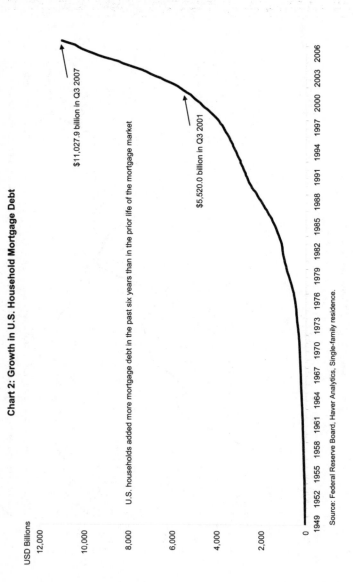

Chart 2: Growth in U.S. Household Mortgage Debt

$11,027.9 billion in Q3 2007

U.S. households added more mortgage debt in the past six years than in the prior life of the mortgage market

$5,520.0 billion in Q3 2001

USD Billions

Source: Federal Reserve Board, Haver Analytics, Single-family residence.

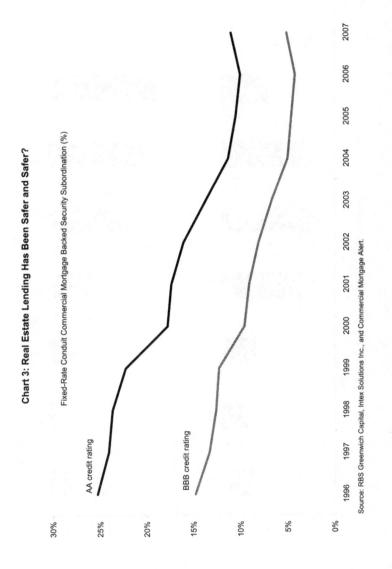

Chart 3: Real Estate Lending Has Been Safer and Safer?

Fixed-Rate Conduit Commercial Mortgage Backed Security Subordination (%)

AA credit rating

BBB credit rating

Source: RBS Greenwich Capital, Intex Solutions Inc., and Commercial Mortgage Alert.

Chart 4: Credit Availability Was Enormous

Subprime Share of Mortgage Originations

2001	2002	2003	2004	2005	2006	2007
7%	7%	8%	18%	20%	20%	11%

Alt-A Share of Mortgage Originations

2001	2002	2003	2004	2005	2006	2007
2%	2%	2%	6%	12%	13%	15%

Source: Inside Mortgage Finance. 2007 to Q2.

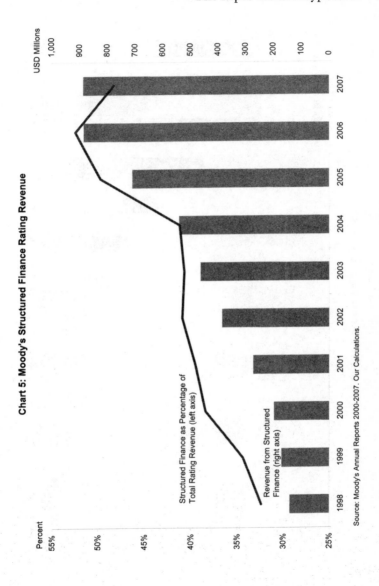

Chart 5: Moody's Structured Finance Rating Revenue

Source: Moody's Annual Reports 2000-2007. Our Calculations.

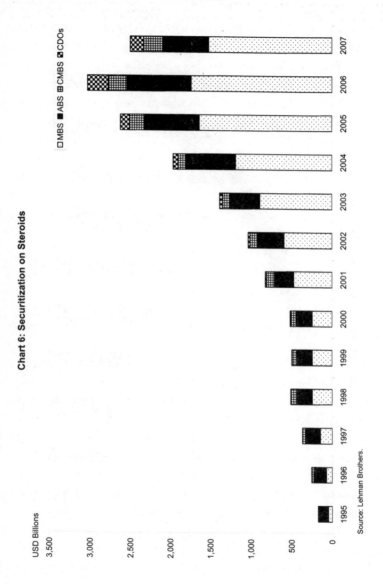

Chart 6: Securitization on Steroids

USD Billions

Source: Lehman Brothers.

sis of 1997. Even so, the stock market recovered from August 2007 to October of that year. That move was not anticipated by my model. The model calls for a collapse that is short and sharp and is followed by a slow and laborious return to near-equilibrium conditions. In this case there was an incomplete give-up in August 2007 and another in January 2008. On each occasion the Fed intervened and lowered the federal funds rate, and the stock market took heart in the belief that the Fed will protect the economy from the consequences of the financial crisis as it has done in the past. I consider that belief misplaced. The Fed is constrained in its ability to protect the economy by the fact that it has done it too often. In my view, this financial crisis is not like the others which have occurred in recent history.

THE SUPER-BUBBLE HYPOTHESIS

Superimposed on the U.S. housing bubble there is a much larger boom-bust sequence which has finally reached its tipping point. The super-bubble is more complex than the housing bubble and requires a more complicated explanation. Boom-bust processes arise out of a reflexive interaction between a prevailing trend and a prevailing misconception. The prevailing trend in the super-bubble is the same as in the housing bubble—ever more sophisticated methods of credit creation—but the misconception is different. It consists of an excessive reliance on the market mechanism. President Ronald Reagan called it the magic of the marketplace. I call it market fundamentalism. It became the dominant creed in

1980 when Reagan became president in the United States and Margaret Thatcher was prime minister in the United Kingdom, although its antecedents go back much further. It was called *laissez-faire* in the nineteenth century.

Market fundamentalism has its roots in the theory of perfect competition, as it was originally propounded by Adam Smith and developed by the classical economists. In the post World War II period it received a powerful fillip from the failures of communism, socialism, and other forms of state intervention. That impetus, however, rests on false premises. The fact that state intervention is always flawed does not make markets perfect. The cardinal contention of the theory of reflexivity is that all human constructs are flawed. Financial markets do not necessarily tend towards equilibrium; left to their own devices they are liable to go to extremes of euphoria and despair. For that reason they are not left to their own devices; they have been put in the charge of financial authorities whose job it is to supervise them and regulate them. Ever since the Great Depression, the authorities have been remarkably successful in avoiding any major breakdown in the international financial system. Ironically, it is their success that has allowed market fundamentalism to revive. When I studied at the London School of Economics in the 1950s, *laissez-faire* seemed to have been buried for good. Yet it came back in the 1980s. Under its influence the financial authorities lost control of financial markets and the super-bubble developed.

The super-bubble combines three major trends, each containing at least one defect. First is the long-term trend towards ever increasing credit expansion as indicated by rising loan-to-value ratios in housing and consumer loans, and rising volume of credit to gross national product ratios (see Chart 7). This trend is the result of the countercyclical policies developed in response to the Great Depression. Every time the banking system is endangered, or a recession looms, the financial authorities intervene, bailing out the endangered institutions and stimulating the economy. Their intervention introduces an asymmetric incentive for credit expansion also known as the moral hazard. The second trend is the globalization of financial markets, and the third is the progressive removal of financial regulations and the accelerating pace of financial innovations. As we shall see, globalization also has an asymmetric structure. It favors the United States and other developed countries at the center of the financial system and penalizes the less-developed economies at the periphery. The disparity between the center and the periphery is not widely recognized, but it has played an important role in the development of the super-bubble. And, as I have already mentioned, both deregulation and many of the recent innovations were based on the false assumption that markets tend towards equilibrium and deviations are random.

The super-bubble ties together the three trends and the three defects. The first trend can be traced back to the 1930s, but the second and third became firmly established only in the 1980s. So one can date the inception of the super-bubble to the 1980s because that is when market fundamentalism became the guiding principle of the international financial system. Clearly, the super-bubble is not a simple process to trace or to explain.

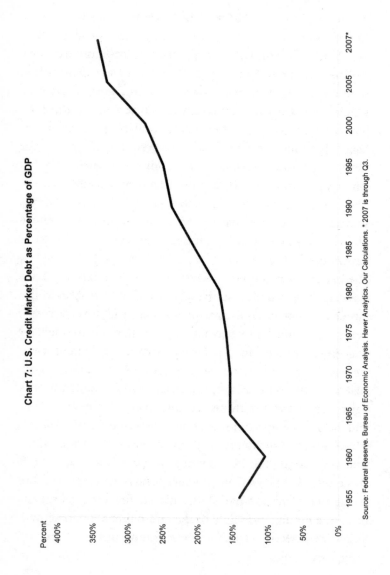

Chart 7: U.S. Credit Market Debt as Percentage of GDP

Source: Federal Reserve. Bureau of Economic Analysis. Haver Analytics. Our Calculations. * 2007 is through Q3.

GLOBALIZATION

The globalization of financial markets was a very success-ful market fundamentalist project. If financial capital is free to move about, it becomes difficult for any state to tax it or to regulate it because it can move somewhere else. This puts fi-nancial capital into a privileged position. Governments often have to pay more heed to the requirements of international capital than to the aspirations of their own people. That is why the globalization of financial markets served the objec-tives of the market fundamentalists so well. The process started with the recycling of petro-dollars in the aftermath of the 1973 oil shock, but it accelerated during the Reagan-Thatcher years.

Globalization did not bring about the level playing field that free markets were supposed to provide according to the market fundamentalist doctrine. The international financial system is under the control of a consortium of financial au-thorities representing the developed countries. They con-stitute the Washington consensus. They seek to impose strict market discipline on individual countries, but they are willing to bend the rules when the financial system itself is endangered. The way the system works, the United States, which enjoys veto power in the Bretton Woods institu-tions—the International Monetary Fund and the World Bank—is "more equal" than others. The dollar has served as the main international reserve currency readily accepted by the central banks of the world. Consequently the United States has been able to pursue countercyclical policies while the developing countries, and to a lesser extent other developed countries, were obliged to live within their means. This has made it safer to hold financial assets at the center than at the periphery. As the barriers to capital movements were removed the savings of the world were sucked up to the center and redistributed from there. In a not-so-strange coincidence, the United States developed a chronic current account deficit in the Reagan years. The deficit has continued to grow ever since, and it reached 6.6 percent of GDP in the third quarter of 2006. The American consumer became the motor of the world economy.

LIBERALIZATION

At the end of World War II the financial industry—banks and markets—was strictly regulated. The postwar years saw the gradual lifting of restrictions, slowly at first, gradually accelerating, and reaching a crescendo in the 1980s. Since financial markets do not tend towards equilibrium, their liberalization gave rise to occasional crises. Most of the crises occurred in the less developed world and could be ascribed to their lack of development, but some endangered the stability of the international financial system, notably the international banking crisis of the 1980s and the emerging market crisis of 1997–1998. In these cases the financial authorities were willing to bend the rules to save the system, but market discipline continued to apply to the less developed world.

This asymmetry, combined with the asymmetric incentive for credit expansion in the developed world, sucked up the savings of the world from the periphery to the center and allowed the United States to develop a chronic current account deficit. Starting in the Reagan years, the United States also developed a large budget deficit. Paradoxically the budget deficit helped to finance the current account deficit because the surplus countries invested their swelling monetary reserves in United States government and agency bonds. This was a perverse situation because capital was flowing from the less-developed world to the United States and both the current account and the budget deficits of the United States served as major sources of credit expansion. Another major source was the introduction of new financial instruments and the increased use of leverage by the banks and some of their customers, notably hedge funds and private equity funds. Yet another source of credit expansion was Japan, which, in the aftermath of a real estate bubble, lowered interest rates to practically zero and is keeping them there indefinitely. This gave rise to the so-called carry trade, whereby foreign institutions borrowed yen, and Japanese individuals used their savings to invest in higher yielding currencies, often on a leveraged basis.

These imbalances could have continued to grow indefinitely because willing lenders and willing borrowers were well matched. There was a symbiotic relationship between the United States, which was happy to consume more than it produced, and China and other Asian exporters, which were happy to produce more than they consumed. The United States accumulated external debt; China and the others accumulated currency reserves. The United States had low savings rates, the others high ones. There was a similar symbiotic relationship between banks and their customers, especially hedge funds and private equity funds, and also between mortgage lenders and borrowers.

The situation became unsustainable with the development of a housing bubble in the U.S. and the introduction of financial innovations based on a false paradigm. Synthetic financial instruments, risk calculations, and proprietary trading models were built on the theory that markets tend toward equilibrium and deviations are random. These innovations took past experience as their starting point, with suitable allowances for deviation and emerging new trends, but they failed to recognize the impact that they, themselves, made. Households became increasingly dependent on the double-digit appreciation in house prices. The savings rate dropped below zero, and households withdrew equity by refinancing their mortgages at an ever increasing rate. Mortgage equity withdrawals reached nearly a trillion dollars in 2006. This was 8 percent of the GDP at its peak, or more than the current account deficit. When house prices stopped rising these trends had to moderate and eventually reverse. Households found themselves overexposed and overindebted. Eventually, consumption had to fall. The bust is following the classic boom-bust pattern, but, in addition, it has also set in motion a flight from the dollar and an unwinding of the other excesses introduced into the financial system by recent innovations. That is how the housing bubble and the super-bubble are connected.

To properly understand what is happening, it is important to realize the difference between this crisis and the periodic crises that have punctuated financial history since the 1980s. The previous crises served as successful tests which reinforced both the prevailing trend and the prevailing misconception of the long-term super-bubble. The current crisis plays a different role: It constitutes the inflection, or tipping point, not only in the housing bubble but also in the long term super-bubble. Those who kept insisting that the subprime crisis was an isolated phenomenon lacked a proper understanding of the situation. The subprime crisis was merely the trigger that released the unwinding of the super-bubble.

While it is clear, in retrospect, that the previous crises played the role of successful tests that reinforced the super-bubble, the role and significance of the current crisis is less clearly defined. My contention that it constitutes the end of an era is just that—a contention, not a fact or a scientific prediction. It needs to be substantiated.

There is considerable evidence to support the super-bubble hypothesis. Credit conditions have been relaxed to such an extent that it is difficult to see how they could be relaxed any further. This is certainly true as far as the U.S. consumer is concerned. Credit terms for mortgages, auto loans, and credit cards have reached their maximum extension. The same is true for some other developed countries, like the United Kingdom and Australia. It may also be true for commercial credit, particularly for leveraged buyouts and commercial real estate. But the same argument could also have been made in connection with previous financial crises. Indeed, I made that argument in *The Crisis of Global Capitalism* at the time of the emerging market crisis of 1997, and I was proven wrong. One cannot predict what new methods of credit creation may be invented and what new sources of funds may be discovered. For instance, in the current crisis a few banks were able to replenish their capital from sovereign wealth funds. Similarly, after the 1987 stock market debacle, Japan emerged as the lender and investor of last resort. In case of need, the Federal Reserve can always print more dollars. So the argument that we have run out of new sources of funds is not fully convincing.

More persuasive is the evidence that this time the crisis is not confined to a particular segment of financial markets but has enveloped the entire financial system. With every passing day it becomes more evident that the current crisis cannot pass as a successful test. The unraveling of markets has defied the efforts of the financial authorities to bring them under control. The central banks have succeeded in pumping liquidity into the banking system, but the flow of credit from the banks to the economy has been disrupted more severely and for a longer period than on any previous occasion. This is the first time since the Great Depression that the international financial system has come close to a genuine meltdown. That is the crucial difference between this financial crisis and previous ones.

What is it that sets the current crisis apart from previous ones? The central banks play the same countercyclical role as before. They were slow to react on this occasion, partly because they may have genuinely believed that the subprime crisis was an isolated phenomenon and partly because they were concerned about the moral hazard. One way or another, they fell behind the curve. But once it became clear that the disruption of the financial sector was going to affect the real economy, the authorities were ready, as always, to provide monetary and fiscal stimulus. Their ability to stimulate the economy is constrained by three factors: First, financial innovation has run amok in recent years, and some of the recently introduced markets and financial instruments have proven unsound and are now unraveling. Second, the willingness of the rest of the world to hold dollars is impaired.

This limits the capacity of the financial authorities to engage in countercyclical policies because these policies could set off a flight from the dollar and raise the specter of runaway inflation. The United States finds itself in a position reminiscent of countries at the periphery. In other words, some of the advantages of being in undisputed control of the system have been lost. Third, the capital base of the banks is severely impaired, and they are unable to get a good grip on their risk exposure. Their first priority is to reduce their exposure. As a result they are unwilling and unable to pass on to their customers the monetary stimulus provided by the Fed. These three factors render an economic slowdown virtually inevitable and turn what should have been a successful test into the end of an era.

The three factors I have identified are closely connected with the three defects which allowed the super-bubble to develop. They are what give the super-bubble its exceptional power. But we must beware of laying too much emphasis on the super-bubble. We must not endow it with magical powers the way President Reagan did with the marketplace. There is nothing predetermined or compulsory about the boom-bust pattern. It is just one manifestation of the reflexive relationships that characterize financial markets, and it does not occur in isolation. Occasionally the pattern becomes so pronounced that it can be studied as if it were an isolated phenomenon. That is the case with the housing bubble, but even there the introduction of synthetic instruments like CDOs (collateralized debt obligations), CDO^2s, and tradable indexes changed the course of events. The super-bubble, as we have seen, is more complicated because it contains other bubbles and the influence of many other factors. I have already mentioned some of them in passing: the commodity boom, the rise of China, etc. I shall deal with them in greater detail when I try to reconstruct the history of the super-bubble. Here I want to caution against the pitfalls that await those who seek to fit the course of events into a predetermined pattern; they are liable to leave many other important factors out of account. The right way to proceed is to fit the pattern to the actual course of events. That is how I arrived at the idea of a super-bubble.

REFLEXIVITY

When I speak of a new paradigm, I do not have the boom-bust pattern in mind; I am referring to the theory of reflexivity. The boom-bust pattern is merely a convincing example of reflexivity. It is convincing because it describes market behavior that is in direct contradiction with the prevailing paradigm, which holds that markets tend towards equilibrium. It ought to be particularly persuasive at the present time, when the markets are in turmoil. The prevailing paradigm cannot explain what is happening; the theory of reflexivity can. The case for abandoning the prevailing paradigm is even stronger: The belief that markets tend towards equilibrium is directly responsible for the current turmoil; it encouraged the regulators to abandon their responsibility and rely on the market mechanism to correct its own excesses. The idea that prices, although they may take random walks, tend to revert to the mean served as the guiding principle for the synthetic financial instruments and investment practices which are currently unraveling.

The theory of reflexivity is different in character from equilibrium theory. Equilibrium theory claims to be a scientific theory in accordance with Karl Popper's model of scientific method. It offers universally valid generalizations that can be used reversibly to provide determinate predictions and explanations similar to the theories of natural science. The theory of reflexivity makes no such claim. It contends that reflexivity, whenever it occurs, introduces an element of indeterminacy into the course of events; therefore it would be inappropriate to look for theories that provide determinate predictions.

I believe that the theory of reflexivity can explain the current states of affairs better than the prevailing paradigm, but I have to admit that it cannot do what the old paradigm did. It cannot offer generalizations in the mold of natural science. It contends that social events are fundamentally different from natural phenomena; they have thinking participants whose biased views and misconceptions introduce an element of uncertainty into the course of events. Events follow a one-directional path that is not determined in advance by universally valid laws, but emerges out of the reflexive interplay between the participants' views and the actual state of affairs. Accordingly the theory of reflexivity can explain events with greater certainty than it can predict the future. That is very different from what we have come to expect from scientific theories. If they recognize reflexivity, social scientists in general and economists in particular need to radically revise the way they interpret the world. That is what has stood in the way of reflexivity becoming the generally accepted paradigm. The severity of the current financial crisis may facilitate a breakthrough.

My theory has been out there for twenty years, but it has not been taken seriously. Even I had doubts about its significance. Admittedly I was not precise and consistent enough in my exposition, and even now I could probably do better. But I no longer have any doubt that the paradigm I am proposing can explain the current state of affairs better than the prevailing one. How far the new paradigm can be developed remains to be seen. There is just so much that one person can do on his own. Others need to get engaged. That is what has prompted me to write this book.

According to the new paradigm, events in financial markets are best interpreted as a form of history. The past is uniquely determined, the future is uncertain. Consequently it is easier to explain how the present position has been reached than it is to predict where it will lead. Currently not one but several reflexive processes are at work at the same time; that renders the range of possibilities exceptionally wide. But explanations also run into difficulties. History, although it is uniquely determined, is so overcrowded that it would be incomprehensible unless the processes and singular events involved were reduced to manageable numbers. That is where the super-bubble hypothesis can be useful. In studying history a hypothesis can help to select the events and developments that deserve consideration.

The super-bubble hypothesis could be used to create a comprehensive financial history of the post–World War II period, culminating in the current crisis. But that is beyond the scope of this book, and my capacity. In the next chapter, however, I substitute for it my experience in the financial markets over the past fifty-five years—a personal history of the time. I think it may be more illuminating than a detailed historical account. After that, I turn to the problem of projecting that experience forward. I record both my outlook at the start of this year and subsequent changes in my views. This real-time experiment is designed to shed light on how my approach works in practice. Following that, I begin a discussion of possible policy responses.

CHAPTER 6

Autobiography of
a Successful Speculator

One of the advantages of having been engaged in the financial markets for more than fifty years is that I have a personal memory of their evolution. In the course of my career I have seen them change out of all recognition. Arrangements that would be outlandish today were at one time accepted as natural, or even unavoidable. And vice versa. Financial instruments and financing techniques that are in widespread use today would have been inconceivable in earlier times. I remember the time when I was an arbitrage trader specializing in warrants and convertible bonds. I was dreaming of creating tradable warrants out of stocks, but of course that would not have been allowed by the regulators. I could not have imagined the range of synthetic instruments that are regularly traded today.

At the end of World War II, the financial industry—banks, brokers, other financial institutions—played a very different role in the economy than they do today. Banks and markets were strictly regulated. The total amount of credit outstanding in relation to the size of the economy was much less than it is today, and the amounts that could be borrowed against different types of collateral were also much smaller. Mortgages required at least 20 percent down payment, and borrowings against stocks were subject to statutory margin requirements that restricted loans to 50 percent or less of the value of the collateral. Auto loans, which required down payment, have been largely replaced by leases, which do not. There were no credit cards and very little unsecured credit. Financial institutions represented only a small percentage of the market capitalization of U.S. stocks. Very few financial stocks were listed on the New York Stock Exchange. Most banks were traded over the counter, and many of them traded only by appointment.

International financial transactions were subject to strict regulation by most countries, and there was very little international capital movement. The Bretton Woods institutions were set up in order to facilitate international trade and to make up for the lack of international investment by the private sector. They were brought into existence by the United States in consultation with a British delegation led by John Maynard Keynes. The British proposed and the United States disposed. The shareholders of the Bretton Woods institutions were the governments of the developed world, but the United States retained veto rights.

Although the international financial system was officially on the gold standard, in effect the dollar served as the international currency. The price of gold was fixed in dollars. For a while the countries of the British Commonwealth remained tied to sterling, but as sterling kept depreciating, the sterling area gradually disintegrated. In the aftermath of the war there was an acute shortage of dollars, and the United States embarked on the Marshall Plan to facilitate the rebuilding of Europe. Gradually the dollar shortage was relieved, and with the formation of the European Common Market and the resurgence of Japan—to be imitated by the Asian tigers—the situation was reversed. Large-scale capital outflows, trade deficits, and the Vietnam War combined to bring the dollar under pressure. But control of the international financial system remained firmly in the hands of the developed countries, with the United States in a dominant position. When the convertibility of the dollar into gold was suspended on August 15, 1971, the dollar remained the main currency in which central banks kept their reserves.

I started my career as a trainee in a London merchant bank in 1954, and learned arbitrage trading in stocks. Arbitrage means trying to take advantage of slight price differences between different markets. International trading at the time was mainly confined to oil and gold stocks, and it required the use of a special type of currency known as switch sterling, or premium dollars. Official exchange rates were fixed, but the currencies used for capital transactions fluctuated beyond the official band according to supply and demand.

I moved to the United States in 1956. After the formation of the European Common Market, there was a lively interest in investing in European securities, and I became actively involved as a trader, security analyst, and salesman. The business came to an abrupt end in 1963 when President John F. Kennedy introduced a so-called interest equalization tax, which effectively imposed a 15 percent surcharge on the purchase of foreign securities abroad. Gradually I shifted my attention to U.S. securities, first as an analyst and then as a hedge fund manager. I belong to the first generation of hedge fund managers. There was not more than a handful of us when I started.

As an analyst I witnessed the gradual awakening of the banking industry. In 1972 I wrote a report entitled "The Case for Growth Banks." Banks at the time were considered the stodgiest of institutions. Managements had been traumatized by the failures of the 1930s, and safety was the paramount consideration, overshadowing profit or growth. The structure of the industry was practically frozen by regulation. Expansion across state lines was prohibited, and in some states even branch banking was outlawed. A dull business attracted dull people, and there was little movement or innovation in the industry. Bank stocks were ignored by investors looking for capital gains.

In my report I argued that conditions were changing, but the changes were not recognized by investors. A new breed of bankers was emerging who had been educated in business schools and thought in terms of bottom-line profits. The spiritual center of the new school of thinking was First National City Bank under the leadership of Walter Wriston, and people trained there were fanning out and occupying top spots at other banks. New kinds of financial instruments were being introduced, and some banks were beginning to utilize their capital more aggressively and putting together very creditable earnings performances. The better banks showed a return on equity in excess of 13 percent. In any other industry, such a return on equity, combined with per-share earnings growth of better than 10 percent, would have been rewarded by the shares selling at a decent premium over asset value, but bank shares were selling at little or no premium. Yet many banks had reached the point where they were pushing against the limits of what was considered prudent leverage by the standards of the time. If they wanted to continue growing they would need to raise additional equity capital. It was against this background that First National City hosted a dinner for security analysts—an unheard-of event in the banking industry.

That is what prompted me to publish my report in which I argued that bank stocks were about to come alive because managements had a good story to tell, and they had started telling it. Bank stocks did, in fact, have a good move in 1972, and I made about 50 percent on the bouquet of growth bank stocks I had bought for my hedge fund.

Then came the first oil shock of 1973, and the money center banks became involved in the recycling of petro-dollars. That is when the Euro-dollar market was born, and the great international lending boom began. Most of the business was conducted abroad, and United States banks formed holding companies to escape regulation at home. Many new financial instruments and financing techniques were invented, and banking became a much more sophisticated business than it had been only a few years earlier. There was a veritable explosion of international credit between 1973 and 1979. It was the foundation of the worldwide inflationary boom of the 1970s. The United States did not participate in the boom. It suffered from stagflation—a combination of rising inflation and high unemployment.

In 1979 a second oil shock reinforced the inflationary pressures. In order to bring inflation under control, the Federal Reserve adopted the monetarist doctrine propounded by Milton Friedman. Instead of controlling short-term interest rates, as it had done hitherto, the Federal Reserve fixed targets for money supply and allowed the rate on federal funds to fluctuate freely. The Federal Reserve's new policy was introduced in October 1979, and interest rates were already at record levels when President Ronald Reagan took office.

President Reagan believed in supply-side economics and a strong military posture. In his first budget, he cut taxes and increased military spending simultaneously. Although a concerted effort was made to reduce domestic spending, the savings were not large enough to offset the other two items. The path of least resistance led to a large budget deficit.

Since the budget deficit had to be financed within the limits of strict money supply targets, interest rates rose to unprecedented heights. Instead of economic expansion, the conflict between fiscal and monetary policy brought on a severe recession. Unexpectedly high interest rates, combined with a recession in the United States, prompted Mexico to threaten defaulting on its international debt obligations in August 1982. That was the inception of the international banking crisis of the 1980s, which devastated Latin America and other developing economies.

The Federal Reserve responded to the crisis by relaxing its grip on the money supply. The budget deficit was just beginning to accelerate. With the brakes released, the economy took off, and the recovery was as vigorous as the recession had been severe. It was aided by a spending spree by both the household and the corporate sectors, and it was abetted by the banking system. Military spending was just gearing up; the household sector enjoyed rising real incomes; the corporate sector benefited from accelerated depreciation and other tax concessions. Banks were eager to lend because practically any new lending had the effect of improving the quality of their loan portfolios. The demand emanating from all these sources was so strong that interest rates, after an initial decline, stabilized at historically high levels and eventually began to rise again. Foreign capital was attracted, partly by the high return on financial assets and partly by the confidence inspired by President Reagan. The dollar strengthened, and a strengthening currency combined with a positive interest rate differential made the move into the dollar irresistible. The strong dollar attracted imports, which helped to satisfy excess demand and to keep down the price level. A self-reinforcing process was set into motion in which a strong economy, a strong currency, a large budget deficit, and a large trade deficit mutually reinforced each other to produce noninflationary growth. In *The Alchemy of Finance* I called this circular relationship Reagan's Imperial Circle because it financed a strong military posture by attracting both goods and capital from abroad. This made the circle benign at the center and vicious at the periphery.* This was the beginning of the United States' current account deficit and the emergence of the United States as consumer of last resort that continued, with many gyrations, to the present day.

The international banking crisis was contained by the active and imaginative intervention of the authorities. Providing liquidity to the banking system was not enough. The amounts owed by sovereign borrowers far exceeded the

---

*I used Reagan's Imperial Circle as an example of a circular reflexive process as distinct from the boom-bust model.

banks' own capital; if the countries in question had been allowed to go into default, the banking system would have become insolvent. The last time that happened was in 1932, and it caused the Great Depression. Because of that experience such an outcome was unacceptable. Accordingly, the central banks exceeded their traditional role and banded together to bail out the debtor countries. A precedent of sorts had been established in England in 1974, when the Bank of England decided to bail out the so-called fringe banks that were outside its sphere of responsibility rather than to allow the clearing banks, from whom the fringe banks had borrowed heavily, to come under suspicion.* But the crisis of 1982 was the first time that the strategy of bailing out the debtors was applied on an international scale.

The central banks did not have sufficient authority to execute such a strategy, and makeshift arrangements had to be made in which the governments of all the creditor countries participated and the International Monetary Fund (IMF) played a key role. Rescue packages were put together for one country after another. Typically, commercial banks extended their commitments, the international monetary institutions injected new cash, and the debtor countries agreed to austerity programs designed to improve their balance of payments. In most cases, the commercial banks also had to come up with additional cash, enabling the debtor countries to stay current on their interest payments. The rescue packages constituted a remarkable achievement in international cooperation. The participants included the IMF, the Bank of International Settlements, a number of governments and central banks, and a

---

*This was, in turn, a precedent for the bailout of Bear Stearns in March 2008.

much larger number of commercial banks. In the case of Mexico, for instance, there were more than five hundred commercial banks involved.

I became a close student of the crisis and its resolution because I was fascinated by the systemic issues involved. I wrote a series of reports, distributed by Morgan Stanley, in which I analyzed the makeshift solution developed by the international financial authorities. I called it the Collective System of Lending. The Collective was held together by the fear of insolvency. Accordingly the integrity of the debt had to be preserved at all costs. That left the debtor countries to fend for themselves; they were granted some concessions on the terms of debt service, but each concession added to their future obligations. The debtor countries accepted this treatment in order to maintain access to capital markets and to avoid seizure of assets and because of fear of the unknown. The austerity programs did improve their trade balances, but in some cases the improvement could not keep pace with the accumulation of debt. Recognizing the problem, banks were building bad debt reserves; but at the time I reviewed the situation in *The Alchemy of Finance*, no way had been found to pass these reserves on to the debtor countries without destroying the principle that held the Collective together. Eventually the problem was solved by the introduction of Brady bonds, but most of Latin America lost a decade of growth.

On previous occasions credit crises led to stricter regulations of the offending entities in order to prevent a recurrence. But under the influence of market fundamentalism, which became the dominant creed in the Reagan years, the international banking crisis led to the opposite outcome:

Banks in the United States were granted greater freedom to make money. Practically all the restrictions that had been imposed on them in the Great Depression were gradually removed. They were allowed to expand their branches, merge across state lines, and enter new lines of business. The separation of investment banking and commercial banking faded until it disappeared altogether. Having been penalized by the Collective System of Lending, banks were anxious to avoid holding loans on their balance sheets; they preferred to package them and sell them off to investors who were not subject to supervision and persuasion by the regulatory authorities. Ever more sophisticated financial instruments were invented, and new ways to keep assets off balance sheets were found. That was when the super-bubble really took off.

The newly invented financial instruments and the newly introduced trading and financing techniques suffered from a fatal flaw. They were based on the assumption that financial markets tend towards equilibrium: They may temporarily deviate from it, but the deviations take the form of a random walk; eventually values revert to the established mean. Accordingly past experience was supposed to provide a reliable guide to the future. This assumption left out of account the impact of the new instruments and new techniques which changed the functioning of financial markets out of all recognition. I could vouch for that from personal experience: When I returned to the markets in the early 1990s after a few years' absence, I could not find my way around.

I date the inception of both globalization and the super-bubble to 1980, when Ronald Reagan and Margaret Thatcher came to power. The period since then was punctuated by occasional breakdowns in particular market segments. The international lending spree of the 1970s turned into the international banking crisis in 1982. The excessive use of portfolio insurance turned a stock market downdraft into an unprecedentedly steep drop in October 1987. Portfolio insurance involved the use of knock-out options. Because they were used on a large scale they could not be exercised without causing a catastrophic discontinuity. Similar episodes occurred on a smaller scale in other markets; I witnessed one in the dollar-yen exchange rate. The slicing up of mortgages into tranches caused a mini crash in the "toxic waste" tranche in 1994, which claimed a few victims. The Russian default in the emerging market crisis of 1998 led to the insolvency of Long-Term Capital Management (LTCM), a very large hedge fund using very high leverage, which threatened the stability of the financial system. It prompted the Fed to lower interest rates and arrange a cooperative rescue of LTCM by its lenders. These incidents did not lead to any regulatory reforms; on the contrary, the ability of the system to withstand these stresses reaffirmed the prevailing market fundamentalist creed and led to further relaxation of the regulatory environment.

Then came the technology bubble that burst in 2000 and the terrorist attack of September 11, 2001. To prevent a recession, the Fed lowered the federal funds rate to 1 percent and kept it there until June 2004. That engendered the housing bubble, in which financial innovations played a major role. With the spreading of risks, more risks could be taken. Unfortunately, the risks were passed on from those who were supposed to know them to others who were less familiar with them. What is worse, the newly invented methods and instruments were so sophisticated that the regulatory authorities lost the ability to calculate the risks involved. They came to depend on the risk control methods developed by the institutions themselves. The latest international agreement on the capital adequacy requirements of banks—Basel 2—allows the largest banks to rely on their own risk management systems. Something similar happened to the rating agencies who were supposed to evaluate the creditworthiness of the financial instruments. They came to rely on the calculations provided by the issuers of those instruments.

I find this the most shocking abdication of responsibility on the part of the regulators. If they could not calculate the risk, they should not have allowed the institutions under their supervision to undertake them. The risk models of the banks were based on the assumption that the system itself is stable. But, contrary to market fundamentalist beliefs, the stability of financial markets is not assured; it has to be actively maintained by the authorities. By relying on the risk calculations of the market participants, the regulators pulled up the anchor and unleashed a period of uncontrolled credit expansion. Specifically, value-at-risk (VAR) calculations are based on past experience. With unchecked credit expansions, the past became a poor guide to current conditions. VAR calculations allowed for two or three standard deviations. Higher standard deviations, which ought to have been extremely scarce, occurred with greater frequency. This ought to have been a warning signal, but it was largely ignored by regulators and participants alike. All they did was to introduce stress tests to measure how well they were prepared for the unexpected.

Similarly, the various synthetic mortgage securities were based on the assumption that the value of houses in the

United States taken as a whole never declines; individual regions may fluctuate, but the market as a whole is stable. That is what made securities spreading the risk over various regions seem more secure than individual mortgages. That assumption ignored the possibility of a nationwide housing bubble of the magnitude that actually occurred.

The regulatory authorities ought to have known better. After all, they had to intervene from time to time, and they knew that their intervention engendered a moral hazard. They paid lip service to the moral hazard, but when the chips were down they came to the rescue of institutions that were too big to fail. They knew that their intervention introduced asymmetric incentives that favored ever-increasing credit expansion, yet they were so carried away by the prevailing market fundamentalist mood and their own success that they came to believe that markets can self-regulate. That is how credit expansion came to reach unsustainable levels.

The right time to constrain credit expansion is during the expansionary phase. Central banks do respond to price and wage inflation but do not feel called upon to prevent asset price inflation.* Alan Greenspan did inveigh against the "irrational exuberance" of the stock market in December 1996 but did not go beyond words and stopped talking about it when his words did not have the desired affect. Greenspan had a more profound understanding of the economic processes than most experts, and he knew how to use the manipulative function in expressing his views. I was impressed by his forward-looking, dynamic approach, which stood in sharp

---

*The Federal Reserve focuses on so-called core prices, excluding energy and food.

contrast to the static, rearview-mirror assessment of European central bankers. He can be faulted, however, for allowing his Ayn Rand–inspired political views to intrude into his conduct as chairman of the Federal Reserve more than would have been appropriate. He supported the Bush tax cuts for the top 1 percent of the population and argued that the budget deficit should be reduced by cutting social services and discretionary spending. And keeping federal funds at 1 percent longer than necessary could have had something to do with the 2004 elections. Responsibility for the real estate bubble can be justly laid at his feet.

Ben Bernanke is more of a theoretician and does not have Greenspan's manipulative skills. He and the Bank of England's Mervyn King were acutely concerned with the moral hazard, and this had much to do with their belated response to the bursting of the housing bubble in 2007. The authorities consistently ignored or underestimated the abuses and excesses in the mortgage industry and their effect on the real economy. That is how the Federal Reserve fell so far behind the curve. The Federal Reserve had the legal authority to regulate the mortgage industry, which it failed to exercise. The Treasury also remained totally passive during this period and became active only when the crisis was well advanced. It introduced new regulations for the mortgage industry only after the industry ground to a standstill, and it confined itself to encouraging voluntary cooperation among lenders to mitigate the damage. That approach had worked in the international banking crisis of the 1980s because central banks could wield direct influence over the commercial banks involved. But the current crisis is incomparably more complicated because the mortgages have been sliced up, repackaged, and resold, and voluntary cooperation among unknown participants is difficult if not impossible to arrange. Treasury Secretary Hank Paulson's attempt to create a so-called super-SIV (structured investment vehicle) to forestall the threat that SIVs would have to dump their assets was still-born; and arrangements to provide relief to people who face a sudden jump in interest payments as their teaser rates expire in the next eighteen months will have only very limited effect. Mortgage service companies are overwhelmed and have no financial incentive to arrange for voluntary restructuring of mortgages. There are some 2.3 million people in that category, many of whom have been duped by unscrupulous lenders. Altogether, the housing crisis will have far-reaching social consequences. One cannot expect the Bush administration to do much about it. It will fall to the next administration to deal with a dismal reality. By that time it will be clearer exactly how dismal it is.

I was watching the evolution of the housing bubble from afar because I was not actively engaged in managing my funds. After my partner who ran the fund left in 2001, I converted my hedge fund into a less aggressively managed vehicle and renamed it an "endowment fund" whose primary task was to manage the assets of my foundations. Most of the money was farmed out to outside managers. Nevertheless, I could clearly see that a super-bubble was developing, and it was bound to end badly. I was on record predicting it in a book published in 2006*. And I was not alone. The investment community was sharply divided between old fogeys

*George Soros, *The Age of Fallibility* (PublicAffairs, 2006).

like me and a younger generation who knew how to use the new instruments and techniques and believed in them. Of course, there were exceptions among them. One of them stood out: John Paulson, who bought insurance against the default of subprime mortgages, which returned a manifold profit on the premium he paid. I invited him to lunch to find out how he did it.

When the crisis erupted in August 2007, I considered the situation grave enough that I did not feel comfortable leaving the management of my fortune to others. I resumed control by establishing a "macro" trading account that gave the fund an overall posture overriding the positions managed by others. I believed that the developed world, particularly the United States, was heading for serious trouble, but there were powerful positive forces at work in other parts of the world, notably China, India, and some of the oil- and raw material–producing countries. We had built up substantial investment positions in the stock markets of those countries. I wanted to protect these positions by establishing substantial short positions in the developed world. I could use only blunt instruments like tradable stock indexes and currencies because I lacked detailed knowledge. Even so, the strategy was reasonably successful. It was not without ups and downs. The market became extremely volatile, and it took a lot of nerve to hold on to the short positions.

CHAPTER 7

My Outlook for 2008

In *The Alchemy of Finance* I conducted a real-time experiment where I documented my decision making as a hedge fund manager at the same time as I was making those decisions. I will repeat the exercise here.

JANUARY 1, 2008

The theory of reflexivity does not offer any firm predictions. It does help, however, to formulate some conjectures on what the future may hold in store.

1. A sixty-year period of credit expansion based on the United States exploiting its position at the center of the global financial system and its control over the international reserve currency has come to an end. The current financial crisis will have more severe and longer-lasting consequences than similar crises in the past. Every crisis involves a temporary credit contraction. The central banks will be able to pro-

vide temporary liquidity, as they did in the past, so that the acute phase of the crisis will be contained as usual; the international banking system will not break down as it did in the 1930s. But on previous occasions each crisis was followed by a new period of economic growth stimulated by easy money and new forms of credit growth. This time it will take much longer for growth to resume. The ability of the Federal Reserve to lower interest rates will be constrained by the unwillingness of the rest of the world to hold dollars and long-term dollar obligations. Some recently introduced financial instruments will have proven unsound and will go out of use. Some major financial institutions may yet prove insolvent, and credit will be harder to get. The extent of credit available for a given collateral will definitely shrink, and its cost will rise. The desire to borrow and take risk is also likely to abate. And one of the major sources of credit expansion, the United States' current account deficit, has definitely peaked. All this is bound to affect the U.S. economy negatively.

2. One can expect some longer-lasting changes in the character of banking and investment banking. These have been growth industries since 1972, launching ever more sophisticated new products and enjoying ever looser regulation. I expect this trend to be reversed. Regulators will try to regain control over the activities of the industry they are supposed to supervise. How far they will go will depend on the severity of the damage. If taxpayers' money is used, Congress will get involved. Finance constituted 14 percent of U.S. stock market capitalization at the end of the 1980s, 15 percent at the end of the 1990s, and peaked at 23 percent in

2006; I expect the percentage to be significantly lower ten years from now. On March 14, 2008, it was 18.2 percent.*

3. There are no grounds, however, for predicting a prolonged period of credit contraction or economic decline in the world as a whole because there are countervailing forces at work. China, India, and some oil-producing countries are experiencing dynamic developments which may not be significantly disrupted by the financial crisis and a recession in the United States. The United States recession itself will be cushioned by an improvement in the current account deficit.

4. The United States during the Bush administration failed to exercise proper political leadership. As a result the United States has suffered a precipitous decline in its power and influence in the world. The invasion of Iraq has much to do with the rise in the price of oil and the unwillingness of the rest of the world to hold dollars. A recession in the United States and the resilience of China, India, and the oil-producing countries will reinforce the decline in the power and influence of the United States. A significant part of the monetary reserves currently held in United States government bonds will be converted into real assets. This will reinforce and extend the current commodity boom and create inflationary pressures. The decline of the dollar as the generally accepted reserve currency will have far-reaching political consequences and raise the specter of a breakdown in the prevailing world order. Generally speaking, we are liable to

*Factset Research Systems Inc (analytical database). Finance includes major banks, regional banks, savings banks, finance leasing, investment banks, investment managers, financial conglomerates, insurance companies, and real estate investment trusts.

pass through a period of great uncertainty and destruction of financial wealth before a new order emerges.

These insights are too general to be of much use in practical decision making, but the theory itself, combined with known facts, does not carry us any further. Indeed, I was pushing the limits to get this far. To be more specific one needs to engage in guesswork.

As we enter the new year I find financial markets too pre-occupied with the liquidity crisis and not sufficiently aware of the long-term consequences. The central banks know how to provide liquidity and will do so, whatever it takes. They have already provided larger amounts against a wider range of collateral than ever before. So the acute phase of the crisis is bound to abate, but the fallout is yet to come. Both investors and the general public suffer from a misconception. They believe that the financial authorities—the Federal Reserve and the administration—will do whatever it takes to avoid a recession. I believe that they are not in a position to do so partly because of the commodity boom and partly because of the vulnerability of the dollar (the two are mutually self-rein-forcing). The world's willingness to hold dollars has been shaken. There are already too many dollars sloshing around, and the holders are eager to diversify. The major alternative reserve currency, the euro, has already been bid up to unsus-tainable levels, yet it is still under upward pressure. The fact that the Chinese renminbi has appreciated less than the euro has created tremendous trade frictions between China and Europe, and something has to give. I believe the renminbi will be allowed to appreciate at a faster rate. The forward premium on the renminbi is already over 8 percent per annum, and I believe the actual appreciation will be higher, although I cannot tell by how much. The Chinese authorities are hard to read, but there are a number of reasons why they should move in that direction. Most important is the threat of protectionism in the United States and now in Europe. An appreciating currency helps to moderate the irritation caused by a large trade surplus. It also helps moderate price inflation, which has become a problem for China. Since the inflation is driven mainly by the cost of imported fuel and food, currency appreciation is a direct antidote. In the past, there was resistance to a higher renminbi from the agricultural sector; with the rise in food prices, that consideration will carry less weight. All this is to the good. But a rising renminbi creates problems which are not properly understood.

The problem for China is that the real cost of capital is already negative, and faster currency appreciation pushes it further into negative territory. This creates an asset bubble. The process is already underway. Real estate is booming, and the Shanghai stock market index appreciated by 97 percent in 2007 and altogether by 420 percent since July 2005* when a four-year bear market ended. For reasons I shall explain in greater detail later, the bubble is still in an early stage, but it may be difficult to avoid a financial crisis later.

The problem for the United States is that a rising renminbi will cause prices at Wal-Mart to rise. A little inflation in a recessionary environment might be a good thing, but the Federal Reserve has to be concerned about the stability of the currency. I believe the Fed will continue to lower interest

---

*420 percent is the percentage change from the low close on July 11, 2005, to end 2007.

rates at a measured pace—1/4 percent every Open Market Committee meeting, probably without interruption—but a point will come when long-term interest rates will rise in response instead of falling. At that point the Fed will have reached the limits of its ability to stimulate the economy. Again, I do not know when this point will be reached, but I suspect it will be sooner rather than later.

There is much uncertainty about the prospect for a recession. Most economic forecasts still rate the chances at less than 50 percent. I cannot understand that. Housing prices will have to fall at least 20 percent over the next five years to get back to a normal relationship to household income. My boom-bust theory tells me that prices have to temporarily fall below the normal relationship in order to clear the market. This means that prices would have to fall by more than 20 percent within a year or so, or the market will not clear for years. At present the market is not clearing, as the latest statistics show. A decline of such magnitude is bound to affect consumer spending, employment, and overall business activity. The only countervailing force is the strength in exports, but that is bound to abate as the rest of the world slows down. Consumer spending has been remarkably resilient, and expectations are definitely erring on the positive side, with 65 percent of house owners expecting the value of their houses to moderately appreciate. My boom-bust theory tells me that participants will have to err on the negative side before the economy can turn positive. Whether we are in a recession now is questionable; that we shall slip into recession in the course of 2008 I consider a certainty.

The unraveling of the financial institutions has not yet run its course either. Year-end results are bound to contain some unpleasant surprises, and a recession is bound to cause further deterioration. There may be some additional shoes to drop. Collateralized debt obligations based on commercial real estate, particularly shopping malls, could easily unravel. Banks sold credit default swaps against their balance sheets, and as the recession progresses there may be some defaults. Markets will not be fully reassured until all the hidden liabilities are fully disclosed. The major investment banks have been very diligent in replenishing their balance sheets by raising capital, mainly from sovereign wealth funds, which hold out the promise of becoming the banking industry's salvation, but their appetite may soon become satiated. This may be yet another case where risks are transferred to those who understand them less well, and the prices paid by the first investors may prove to have been too high.

Europe is liable to be affected almost as badly as the United States. Spain, with its own real estate bubble, and the United Kingdom, given the importance of London as a financial center, are particularly vulnerable. European banks and pension funds are even more heavily weighed down with assets of doubtful value than American banks, and the overvaluation of the euro and sterling is going to hurt European economies. The Japanese economy is also doing poorly. The developed countries, taken together, make up 70 percent of the world economy. Nevertheless, I question whether the global economy will go into recession because of the very favorable dynamics that prevail in the oil-rich countries and some of the developing economies. Conventional wisdom says that when the United States sneezes the rest of the world catches cold. That used to be true, but no longer.

China is undergoing a radical structural transformation, and the asset bubble engendered by negative real interest rates is facilitating the process. State-owned enterprises are being transferred into private hands, and managements usually end up with significant stakes. Skillful managers used to make money on the side; now they find it advantageous to make money for the companies they manage and, to an increasing extent, own. Stocks listed on the Shanghai Stock Exchange may appear overvalued by conventional yardsticks (over forty times next year's earnings), but appearances may be deceptive when the motivation of management changes. No doubt a bubble is in formation, but it is in a relatively early stage, and there are powerful interests at work to keep the bubble going. The economic elite are eager to convert the perks of office they currently enjoy into ownership of property that they can pass on to their heirs. There is a long queue of companies whose managers are eager to get rid of state ownership, and they do not want to see the process interrupted. Nothing is quite as profitable as investing in an early-stage bubble.

I visited China in October 2005, and although I was no longer actively making investments, I saw greater opportunities there than at any time in my career. The Chinese economy had been growing at better than 10 percent a year over the past decade, but corporate earnings were not keeping pace with growth, and, after the initial euphoria that is characteristic of newly established stock markets, stocks had been in a bear market for the preceding four years. The government had just announced a scheme whereby all state-owned shares would become tradable within twenty-four months. I saw the opportunity of a lifetime, but I was not willing to go back into active money management, and I could not find a suitable Chinese partner. We did put some money to work in China, but, as always in these cases, not enough. The Shanghai index has risen by more than 400 percent since then.

China is exerting considerable influence on other emerging economies. It has shown an insatiable appetite for raw materials, and it has been the main motor of the boom in commodities and dry cargo shipping. In spite of the expected slowdown in the world economy, the price for iron ore is expected to rise at least 30 percent next year, with China as the largest customer. China has embarked on a shopping spree for mining, oil, and other raw material–producing companies. It is also ready to extend long-term credit on concessionary rates to African countries. It has come to rival the West as the source of capital inflows into Africa. China has also become the major trading partner of many Asian countries. (It is also becoming the largest producer of greenhouse gases in the world, but that is not the topic of discussion here.)

Undoubtedly, the recession in the developed world will adversely affect Chinese exports, but the domestic economy, and investments in and exports to the developing world, could take up much of the slack. The rate of growth will slow down, but the bubble, fueled by negative real interest rates, will continue to grow. The stock market index will certainly not continue to rise at the rate at which it did last year. Indeed, it may not rise at all, but the volume of new issues and the total size of the market will continue to grow unabated. The structural transformation of the economy will become more pronounced. Loss-making state-owned enterprises will more or less disappear, and what I call super state-owned enterprises—spin-offs from state-owned enterprises which are well managed and justify their high stock prices by absorbing additional assets from their mother company—will become a dominant feature of the market. The process will be somewhat similar to what I described as merger mania in the chapter "The 'Oligopolarization' of America" in *The Alchemy of Finance*, but much more dramatic. It may or may not come to a bad end, but in any case the end is several years away. In my judgment, China will sail through the current financial crisis and subsequent recession with flying colors and gain considerable relative strength.

The longer-term outlook for China is highly uncertain. It would not be surprising if the currently developing bubble ended in a financial crisis several years down the road. I said long ago that communism in China is likely to be brought to an end by a capitalist crisis. Alternatively, the transformation of China into a capitalist economy may be accomplished without a financial crisis. Either way, China is likely to challenge the supremacy of the United States much sooner than could have been expected when George W. Bush was elected president. What an ironic outcome for the Project for a New American Century! How to accommodate a surging China within the world order will be one of the most challenging tasks for the incoming administration.

I visited India at Christmastime in 2006, and I was even more positively impressed from an investment point of view than with China because India is a democracy with the rule of law. Moreover, it was technically easier to invest in India than in China. Market averages have more than doubled since that time. India used to grow at 3.5 percent per annum, barely higher than the population growth. The growth rate has now more than doubled. The groundwork of economic reforms was laid by the present prime minister, Manmohan Singh, when he was finance minister more than a decade ago, and it took some time for the dynamics of the economy to change. Information technology outsourcing served as the catalyst. Its growth was phenomenal. Last year India accounted for more than half the new jobs in that industry worldwide, but even today it represents less than 1 percent of total employment in India. The industry has passed its peak of profitability. There is a shortage of qualified labor, and profit margins are hurt by the appreciation of the currency. But the dynamics have spread to the rest of the economy.

The most spectacular has been the rise of the Ambani brothers. When their father, the founder of Reliance Industries, died, the brothers divided his empire among them and are now trying to outdo each other. Their activities range from oil refining, petrochemicals, and offshore natural gas production, to financial services and cellular telephones. The discovery of offshore natural gas promises to make India energy self-sufficient within the next few years. Mukesh Ambani is using the cash flow from his oil and gas business to set up Reliance Retail, bringing food directly from the grower to the consumer—a bold project that seeks to cut the differential between consumer and producer prices by more than half.

India's infrastructure lags far behind China's, but infrastructure investment is beginning to pick up, helped by domestic savings and capital inflows from the oil-rich Gulf States, which have large expatriate Indian populations. In these circumstances, I expect the Indian economy to perform well, although, after its stellar performance, the stock market may be vulnerable to correction.

Another source of strength for the world economy is to be found in some of the oil-producing countries of the Middle East (I don't discuss Russia because I don't want to invest there). These states are accumulating reserves at an impressive rate, by $122 billion in 2006 and by an estimated $114 billion in 2007, to a reserve level of $545 billion.* They are eager to diversify out of dollar denominated bonds and have all set up sovereign wealth funds whose assets are growing rapidly. The Gulf States have decided to invest in developing their own economies by exploiting their access to cheap energy, building oil refining and petrochemical plants, aluminum smelters, and other heavy industries at a rate which is limited only by the shortage of labor and equipment. Due to their competitive advantage, they are likely to become dominant factors in these industries. Abu Dhabi has decided to establish a metropolis to rival Dubai. With over a trillion dollars in reserves and a population of 1.6 million (80 percent are expatriates), they can afford to do so. The forced pace of development has created inflationary pressures and there is a strong case for unpegging the currencies from the dollar. Kuwait has already done so, but the other states, particularly Saudi Arabia, have been dissuaded from following Kuwait's example by strong political pressure from Washington. The dollar pegs, coupled with domestic inflation, have brought about negative real interest rates. The stock markets of the Gulf States are emerging from a severe crash that followed

---

*International Monetary Fund World Economic and Financial Surveys, October 2007. The countries behind these numbers include: Bahrain, Iran, Iraq, Kuwait, Libya, Oman, Qatar, Saudi Arabia, and the United Arab Emirates. Saudi Arabia's gross reserves include investments in foreign securities, which are excluded in the reporting of official reserves.

the initial euphoria, and negative real interest rates are attracting capital inflows from abroad, just as in China. That is the perverse effect of dollar pegs, although in the case of the Gulf States—with the exception of Kuwait—the peg is not crawling. I believe the dynamics are strong enough—despite the political risks posed by Iran—to withstand a worldwide slowdown. Any lowering of interest rates in the United States would increase the pressure to break the peg.

Sovereign wealth funds are becoming important players in the international financial system. Their current size is estimated at about $2.5 trillion, and they are growing rapidly. They have already invested $28.65 billion in ailing financial institutions.* China has allocated $5 billion to investing in Africa. Sovereign wealth funds are likely to emerge as lenders and investors of last resort similar to the role that Japan sought to play after the stock market crash of 1987. But the sovereign wealth funds are more diverse than the Japanese financial institutions were, and they are likely to follow divergent paths. The financial crisis is likely to make them more welcome in the West than they would have been otherwise. It will be recalled that a Chinese state-owned oil company, China National Offshore Oil Corporation, ran into political opposition when it tried to acquire Unocal, as did a Dubai company, DP World, when it sought to take control of American port facilities. To the extent that one can generalize, sovereign wealth funds are likely to favor investing in the developing world,

---

*July 13, 2007, Temasek Holdings, $2.0 billion in Barclays PLC; November 26, 2007, Abu Dhabi Investment Authority, $7.5 billion in Citigroup Inc.; December 10, 2007, Government of Singapore Investment Corp., $9.75 billion in UBS AG; December 19, 2007, China Investment Corp. $5.0 billion in Morgan Stanley; December 24, 2007, Temasek Holdings, at least $4.4 billion in Merrill Lynch.

limited only by the absorptive capacity of those countries. That is likely to reinforce the positive performance of the developing economies. Sovereign wealth funds are also likely to become significant stakeholders in the United States economy unless prevented by protectionist measures.

Whether the global slowdown will turn into a global recession is an open question. One can, however, predict with a fair degree of certainty that the developing world will perform much better than the developed countries. This may set up an eventual reversal, when the investments in raw material production will have created overcapacity.

In 2007, being long in emerging markets and short in the stock markets of the developed world was a rewarding investment strategy. I expect that this will continue to be the case in 2008 but with a significant shift of emphasis from being net long to being net short. Due to the change in character of my fund from a pure hedge fund to an endowment fund, and my reduced role in managing it, I do not consider it appropriate to give a detailed account of our investment positions as I did in the real-time experiment published in *The Alchemy of Finance*. I can, however, summarize my investment strategy for 2008 in one sentence: short U.S. and European stocks, U.S. ten-year government bonds, and the U.S. dollar; long Chinese, Indian, and Gulf States stocks and non-U.S. currencies.

JANUARY 6, 2008

The real-time experiment is off to a better start than I expected. We are making money both with our longs and shorts, and currencies. Only our short position in ten-year

U.S. government bonds is working against us, but this was to be expected; bonds and stocks tend to move in opposite directions. I took on the position knowing that I may be early, but with a depreciating dollar I believe it will eventually prove to be right, and in the meantime it reduces the volatility of the portfolio. In keeping with our character of an endowment fund rather than a regular hedge fund, our exposure is relatively modest: less than half our equity in any one direction. Nevertheless, the fund is up more than 3 percent in three trading days.

I started thinking about when to cover my short positions. Certainly not yet. The market has just started to recognize that a recession is in store; it has to fall below the lows of 2007. For the next six months the surprises are likely to be on the negative side. I do not expect this administration to be capable of producing any policy measures that would meaningfully improve the situation. The market may, of course, establish a tradable bottom sooner than six months—I am not very good at picking bottoms.

MARCH 10, 2008

I got the big picture right in my predictions for 2008, but there were some minor deviations which have had a major impact both on the course of events and on our investment performance.

- The disruption of the financial system has been worse than I expected. Markets that I did not even know existed—such as the auction-rated municipal bond market—fell apart.

Credit spreads continued to widen, and losses continued to mount. Banks and brokers have recently raised their margin requirements, and leveraged hedge funds are forced to deleverage. Some are being liquidated. There are still some shoes left to drop; the gigantic credit default swap market has yet to unravel. Write-offs are likely to peak in the first quarter of 2008. There may be further losses in later quarters, but not at the same rate.

- Commodity markets stayed stronger than I expected. The rise in iron ore prices was 60 percent, not 30 percent. Gold is approaching $1,000 an ounce.
- The Federal Reserve swung around more violently than I expected. It dropped the federal funds rate by an unprecedented three-quarter percent in an emergency meeting on January 22 and moved another half percent at its regular meeting on January 30.
- In spite of its dramatic turnaround, the Fed was unable to bring down mortgage rates, but for a different reason than the one I anticipated. It was the widening of credit spreads, not the steepening of the yield curve, that pushed up mortgage rates. The yield on ten-year government bonds dropped sharply, and our short position turned out to be very costly.
- The Indian market had a big fall. We had failed to cut back on our long positions and took it on the chin. Losses in these two positions (China has not hurt us much) offset most of our gains in the macro-account. As a result we are barely ahead for the year.

Having increased our short positions in the dollar and in U.S. and European stock indexes and financial stocks, and slightly reduced our government bond shorts, we seem to be well positioned for the period immediately ahead. I expect a re-test of the January stock market bottom with financial stocks making new lows but the market as a whole holding above. This may lead to a tradable rally, but I foresee lower lows in the months ahead.

A new chief investment officer joined me recently; this will allow me to distance myself from the markets. We intend to cover some or most of our financial shorts in the re-test and maybe go long in some stocks that will benefit from a lower dollar and then establish new shorts on the rally. The new CIO knows the bond markets well. He is accumulating some of the higher-grade mortgage indexes and intends to increase our shorts in long-term government bonds in due course.

MARCH 16, 2008

This has been a dramatic week. The deleveraging of hedge funds continued, and some are being forcibly liquidated, putting downward pressure on securities and upward pressure on credit spreads. The dollar is making new lows, with the euro breaking through $1.55 and the yen breaking 100 to the dollar. Pressures in the currency markets are intensifying. Both the Chinese and the Gulf currencies are straining against their dollar pegs. On Thursday, Bear Stearns came under suspicion as a counterparty, forcing the Fed to come to the rescue on Friday by opening the credit window to Bear through the intermediation of JP Morgan. The panic is palpable. We continued to add to the dollar shorts, but we started going against the decline in the stock market and the continued rise in government bonds. We also bought some Bear Stearns shares and sold some Bear Stearns credit default swaps on Friday (the first time we traded in that market) in the expectation that Bear Stearns will be auctioned off by the Fed over the weekend. This is a short-term, finite bet that either pays off on Monday or has to be taken off the table. The result to date is a standoff; the fund continues to tread water, with the macro-account making money and the rest of the fund losing. Our only consolation is that the portfolio is much less volatile than the markets. It would be better to show a profit.

MARCH 20, 2008

Another eventful week. Bear Stearns was not auctioned off but forced into the hands of JP Morgan at $2 a share. We were half right: made money on the credit default swaps but lost on the shares—a wash. The shareholders of Bear are squealing, but are probably powerless. We forgot to take into account that Bear is disliked by the establishment, and the Fed would use the occasion to deal with the moral hazard by punishing the shareholders.

The markets were shocked by the Fed's action, and we had some kind of a selling climax on Monday. We used the occasion to cover our remaining shorts in financial stocks, and we were almost neutral in our stock exposure by Tuesday morning, betting that Lehman Brothers, which came under siege on Monday, would be able to withstand the onslaught. We were right, and after the Fed cut rates by another 75 basis points stocks staged the best rally of the year. This ought to have been a tradable rally, lasting at least a few weeks, but the stock market broke all the rules and reversed itself on Wednesday. In every boom-bust sequence people come to believe that the normal rules do not apply, but they usually do. This time it really is different, confirming my thesis that this crisis is not like the other ones. To top it off, the dollar staged a sharp rally on Thursday morning, causing some damage to the macro-account. The fund is now under water for the year. I ascribe the dollar rally to the liquidation of speculative positions, some forced and some technical. I intend to hold my positions, but I am prepared to see further losses. One of the advantages of low leverage is that I can afford it.

I have to end the real-time experiment because the manuscript has to go to the publisher. I would have preferred to end it with a profit for the overall fund, not just the macro-account, but this result may be more appropriate for the purposes of this book. We are in a period of forced deleveraging and the destruction of financial wealth. It is difficult to escape it.

MARCH 23, 2008

In writing the conclusion to my book I gained a new insight into what is to be expected for the rest of 2008. It will guide my investment decisions. I shall conclude the real-time experiment by quoting the key passage:

Eventually, the U.S. government will have to use taxpayers' money to arrest the decline in house prices. Until it does, the decline will be self-reinforcing, with people

walking away from homes in which they have negative
equity and more and more financial institutions becoming insolvent, thus reinforcing both the recession and
flight from the dollar. The Bush administration and
most economic forecasters do not understand that markets can be self-reinforcing on the downside as well as
the upside. They are waiting for the housing market to
find a bottom on its own, but it is further away than they
think.

S&P/Case-Shiller Home Price Index
20-City Composite, Y/Y%, through January

Source: S&P/Case-Shiller Home Price Index, March 25, 2008.

CHAPTER 8

Some Policy Recommendations

It would be premature to put forward firm policy recommendations for several reasons. First, I am too involved in the markets to give the matter serious consideration. The drama currently unfolding is all-absorbing, and I have a lot at stake. I shall have to distance myself from the market to be able to think in a more detached manner. Second, not much can be expected from the current administration. Major new initiatives will have to await the new president, and only a Democratic president can be expected to turn things around and lead the nation in a new direction. Third, the situation is very serious, and the new policy initiatives need to be thoroughly discussed. I shall outline my current thinking more as subjects for discussion than as firm conclusions.

Clearly an unleashed and unhinged financial industry is wreaking havoc with the economy. It needs to be reined in. Credit creation by its nature is a reflexive process. It needs to be regulated in order to prevent excesses. We must remember, however, that regulators are not only human but also bureaucratic. Going overboard with regulations could severely impede economic activity. A return to the conditions that prevailed after World War II would be a big mistake. Credit availability fosters not only productivity but also flexibility and innovation. Credit creation should not be put into a straitjacket. The world is full of uncertainty, and markets can adjust to changing conditions much better than bureaucrats. At the same time, we must recognize that markets do not just passively adjust to changing circumstances but also actively contribute to shaping the course of events. They may create the instabilities and uncertainties that make their flexibility so valuable. This has to be taken into account in formulating macroeconomic policies. Markets should be given the greatest possible scope compatible with maintaining economic stability.

In large part the excesses in the financial markets are due to the regulators' failure to exercise proper control. Some of the newly introduced financial instruments and methods were based on false premises. They have shown themselves to be unsustainable, and therefore they will have to be abandoned. But others help to spread or hedge against risks and need to be preserved. The regulators need to gain a better understanding of the recent innovations, and they ought not to allow practices that they do not fully understand. The idea that risk management can be left to the participants was an aberration. There are systemic risks that need to be managed by the regulatory authorities. To be able to do so they must have adequate information. The participants, including hedge funds and sovereign wealth funds and other unregulated entities, must provide that information even if it is costly and cumbersome. The costs pale into insignificance when compared to the costs of a breakdown.

Moral hazard poses a thorny problem, but it can be resolved. Let's face it: When the financial system is endangered, the authorities must cave in. Whether they like it or not, institutions engaged in credit creation must accept the fact that they are being protected by the authorities. They must, therefore, pay a price for it. The authorities must exercise more vigilance and control during the expansionary phase. That will undoubtedly limit the profitability of the business. The people engaged in the business will not like it and will lobby against it, but credit creation has to be a regulated business. Regulators ought to be held accountable if they allow matters to get out of hand so that an institution has to be rescued. In recent years matters did get out of hand. The financial industry was allowed to get far too profitable and far too big.

The most important lesson to be learned from the current crisis is that the monetary authorities have to be concerned not only with controlling the money supply but also with credit creation. Monetarism is a false doctrine. Money and credit do not go hand in hand. Monetary authorities have to be concerned not only with wage inflation but also with avoiding asset bubbles. Asset prices depend not only on the availability of money but also on the willingness to lend. The monetary authorities have to monitor and take into account not only money supply but also credit conditions. It will be objected that asking the monetary authorities to control asset prices gives them one too many tasks to perform. The objection would be valid if the task of the monetary authorities could be confined to applying certain rules mechanically. Their job is more complicated than that. They are engaged in a delicate game of managing expectations using all the tricks involved in the exercise of the manipulative function. That is an art, and it cannot be reduced to science. Alan Greenspan was a grand master of the manipulative function. Unfortunately he put his skills at the service of the wrong cause; he was too much of a market fundamentalist.

Both the housing bubble and the super-bubble have been characterized by the excessive use of leverage. This was supported by sophisticated risk management models that calculated known risks but ignored the uncertainties inherent in reflexivity. If they do nothing else, regulators must reassert control over the use of leverage. They used to exercise such control. Equities are still subject to margin requirements, although these have become largely meaningless because there are so many ways around them. Mortgage securities and other synthetic instruments were never brought under control because they were introduced during the market fundamentalist era. Controlling leverage will reduce both the size and the profitability of the financial industry, but that is what the public interest demands.

One specific measure that could help relieve the credit crisis is the establishment of a clearing house or exchange for credit default swaps. Forty-five trillion dollars worth of contracts are outstanding and those who hold the contracts do not know whether their counterparties have adequately protected themselves. If and when defaults occur some of the counterparties are likely to prove unable to fulfill their obligations. This prospect overhangs the market like a Sword of Damocles that is bound to fall, but not yet. It must have played a role in the Fed's decision not to allow Bear Stearns to fail. There is much to be gained by establishing a clearing house or exchange with a sound capital structure and strict margin requirements to which all existing and future contracts would have to be submitted.

What is to be done about the mess created by the bursting of the housing bubble? The usual anti-cyclical monetary and fiscal policies are appropriate as far as they go, but for the reasons I have given, they will not go far enough. Additional measures are needed to contain the collapse in house prices and alleviate the pain connected with it. For both these reasons it is desirable to let as many people keep their homes as possible. This applies both to the holders of subprime mortgages and to the people whose mortgages exceed the value of their houses. They may be considered victims of the housing bubble deserving some relief. But giving them relief is tricky because mortgages derive their value from the fact that they can be enforced by foreclosure. In most other countries borrowers are personally liable, while in the United States lenders usually have no recourse other than foreclosure. On the other hand, foreclosures depress house prices and aggravate the slump. They are also costly to all parties involved and result in negative spillover effects. What can be done to balance these considerations? This is a subject to which I have given more detailed consideration than the other issues I have discussed so far, and I have also involved my foundation, the Open Society Institute. Here are my preliminary findings.

About 40 percent of the 7 million subprime loans outstanding will default in the next two years. The defaults of option-adjustable-rate mortgages and other mortgages subject to rate reset will be of the same order of magnitude but over a somewhat longer period of time. This will maintain the downward pressure on house prices. Prices are likely to fall below the long-term trend unless arrested by government intervention.

The human suffering caused by the housing crisis will be enormous. There is significant evidence that senior citizens were targeted for some of the worst predatory practices and are disproportionately defaulting on their mortgages. Communities of color are also disproportionately affected. Given that home ownership is a key factor in increasing wealth and opportunity in the United States, upwardly mobile young professionals of color will be particularly hard hit. They bought into the promise of the "ownership society," and their assets are concentrated in home ownership. Prince George's County, Maryland, offers a prime example. It is one of the most prosperous predominantly black counties in the nation, yet it is experiencing the highest number of foreclosures in Maryland. Data for Maryland show that 54 percent of African American homeowners have subprime loans, compared to 47 percent for Hispanics and 18 percent for Whites.

Foreclosures reduce the value of surrounding houses, pushing additional home owners to abandon their property because their mortgages exceed the values of their houses. Ultimately, concentrated foreclosures destabilize entire neighborhoods and have repercussions in other areas, such as employment, education, health, and child well-being. Avoiding foreclosure ought to be the primary focus of additional policy measures. The already enacted initiatives of the Bush administration do not amount to more than exercises in public relations. Once you apply all the limitations you are left with practically nothing.

Both systemic and individualized approaches are needed. As regards the need for systemic intervention, I believe that

Representative Barney Frank is on the right track, although in order to gain bipartisan support he does not go far enough. He put forward two proposals that would strike the right balance between protecting the right to foreclosure and discouraging the exercise of that right—if they were adopted in the sequence that he proposes. First, he would modify the bankruptcy law so that a bankruptcy judge could rewrite mortgage loan terms on a principal residence. This would put pressure on the lenders to voluntarily modify such mortgages in order to avoid a compulsory modification of the mortgage, or a "cram down." The objection from the Republican side is that it would impinge on the rights of the lender and therefore make mortgages more expensive in the future. But the Frank proposal only applies to mortgages originated between January 2005 and June 2007. Moreover, the current bankruptcy law already allows modifications of mortgages on second homes, and it has not affected their cost appreciably.

Second, Frank would empower the Federal Housing Administration (FHA) to provide guarantees that would help refinance subprime borrowers into affordable mortgages. The holders of the original loan would be paid off from the proceeds of a new FHA-insured loan at no more than 85 percent of the current appraised value of the house. To compensate the FHA for providing guarantees, the FHA would retain a second lien on the property. When the borrower sells the home or refinances the loan, the borrower will pay from any profit of the higher of (1) an ongoing exit fee equal to 3 percent of the original FHA loan balance; or (2) a declining percentage of any profits (e.g., from 100 percent in year one to 20 percent in year five and 0 percent thereafter). After year five, only the 3 percent exit fee will apply.

Both the strength and the weakness of this proposal is that it is voluntary. On the positive side, it does not violate the right to foreclosure. On the negative side, it applies only to a rather narrow segment of troubled mortgages. It is confined to borrowers whose income is at least two-and-a-half times their debt service costs. At the same time, the mortgage holders must be willing to accept 85 percent of the current market value as payment in full without participating in any potential future upside in the home value. Frank's FHA proposal may well pass into law under the Bush administration but it is unlikely to have much impact on the housing crisis. It will have to be substantially enlarged before it makes a meaningful difference. The bankruptcy modification, by contrast, would be meaningful, but it is opposed by the Bush administration.

According to the mortgage industry, there are a number of legal and practical impediments that prevent loan servicers from modifying subprime loans facing delinquency and default. Servicers argue that securitization of mortgages makes it difficult to track individual loans and that "pooling and servicing agreements" substantially limit their discretion to alter loan terms. But the main impediment is "tranche warfare." Different tranches have competing interests in a given loan—one tranche may have a priority claim to the principal, another to the interest. Servicers resist rewriting mortgages because one tranche inevitably will take a deeper hit than others, and servicers are accountable to all tranches simultaneously.

There is a growing consensus, however, that pooling and servicing agreements allow greater flexibility than previously acknowledged. Notwithstanding the problems of securitizations, Moody's confirms that the rate of loan modifications is on the rise, but it still accounted for only 3.5 percent of the loans that reset in 2007. More attention should be devoted to quantifying and documenting the benefits of loan modifications in order to persuade lenders to put additional pressure on their servicers to engage in workouts.

Unfortunately, however, even with sweeping reforms, many homeowners will be unable to afford to stay in their homes. Local governments will need to come to terms with the fact that a significant share of homeowners will lose their homes. And because the most unscrupulous lending was concentrated in communities of color, which are the most vulnerable financially, local governments face the daunting prospect of huge inventories of distressed properties being dumped on the market in precisely those neighborhoods least equipped to absorb the shock. The trick here will be to ensure that those properties do not fall vacant or into the hands of absentee owners, but rather are quickly transferred to responsible buyers who occupy and maintain their homes.

Helping local communities will be a fertile field for private philanthropy. Matching funds from the federal and state governments could greatly increase its scope and impact. My foundation is sponsoring local initiatives in New York City and Maryland.

In New York City, we have initiated the Center for New York City Neighborhoods with funding from New York City government, private philanthropy, and the lending industry. It will increase and coordinate foreclosure prevention advocacy, including counseling and referral services, legal assistance, loan remediation, and preventive outreach and education. Its primary mission is to keep borrowers in their homes. For those who are unable to stay in their homes, it will support the efficient transfer of properties to responsible homeowners or nonprofit organizations to ensure neighborhood stability. We are hopeful that it will assist as many as eighteen thousand borrowers annually. The Center for New York City Neighborhoods will serve as an honest broker, facilitating communication among borrowers, direct service providers, and the lending industry. Although New York City's housing market has not been hardest hit by the current crisis, I hope that local solutions piloted in New York will serve as a model for other communities.

Various efforts are underway in Maryland to assist homeowners in or near default on their mortgages. The Baltimore Homeownership Preservation Coalition and a similar coalition in Prince George's County offer homeowners in trouble a place they can turn to which has their best interests at heart. The limiting factor is the lack of well-trained counselors. We plan to support various training schemes, some of which will likely receive state support.

We are studying what else can be done.

PART III

The Crash of 2008 and What it Means

CHAPTER 9

The Crash of 2008

INTRODUCTION

In the previous edition of this book, I put forward a conceptual framework for understanding the financial crisis then beginning to unfold. I recognized that the crisis was more severe than many were willing to accept, but even I never expected the financial system to actually break down and the global economy to collapse. In the past, whenever we came to the brink of a breakdown the financial authorities came to the rescue. That is what I expected for 2008, but that is not what happened. On September 15, 2008, Lehman Brothers was allowed to go into bankruptcy without proper preparation. Within days the entire financial system suffered what amounted to cardiac arrest and had to be put on artificial life support. The effect on the global economy was the equivalent of the collapse of the banking system during the Great Depression. The current breakdown is a relatively recent event whose full impact has not yet been felt, and it contradicts my explicitly stated expectations for 2008. In sum, I significantly underestimated the severity of the financial crisis. I was correct, however, in identifying that we were dealing with something much bigger than a subprime mortgage crisis or a housing bubble and that we had reached the reversal point in a process of credit expansion that had been at work ever since World War II and turned into a super-bubble in the 1980s.

Recognizing this point is essential for understanding where we are now and what policies we should follow, and for evaluating the conceptual framework I have put forward. In the following pages, I shall assess the present state of affairs first and the conceptual framework afterwards. I shall use my own investment performance to set the stage for reviewing the salient events of 2008 and then turn to the policy prescriptions.

Performance Evaluation

On rereading chapter 7, "My Outlook for 2008," it is clear that by and large I foresaw what was coming and positioned myself reasonably well in anticipation. But I got one thing wrong and it cost me dearly: There was no decoupling between the developed and developing worlds. The Indian and Chinese stock markets were hit even harder than those in the United States and Europe. Since we did not reduce our exposure, we lost even more money in India than we made the year before. Our Chinese manager did better than the market through his stock selection; we were also helped by the appreciation of the Chinese currency. I had to push very hard in my macro-account to offset these losses and the losses incurred by our external managers. This had its own drawback: I overtraded. The positions I took were too large for the increasingly volatile markets, and in order to manage my risk I could not afford to go against the trend in a major way. I had to try and catch minor market moves, and this made it difficult to maintain short positions.

The risk-reward relationship in selling stocks short is the exact opposite of being long. If you are long and the market goes against you, your risk exposure goes down. If you are short it goes up. As a result, short sellers cannot tolerate losses the way investors can. Because the short side was crowded, there were some vicious short-squeezes. Although I am an experienced short seller, I got caught several times, and in the end I largely missed the biggest downdraft, which came in October and November.

The increased volatility was an expression of the increased uncertainty. That was a point I made in the conclusion to last year's book, where I spoke of a period of heightened uncertainty but failed to draw the right conclusion for my trading tactics. Had I kept my risk exposure lower, I could have stuck to my strategic positions, and I might have ended up making more money.

I say "might have" rather than "would have" because although I was heavily weighted on the short side, the few strategic long positions I took on cost me an enormous amount. I was impressed by the potential in the newly discovered deep-water oil field in Brazil in light of the rapid depletion of existing major oil fields and bought a large, strategic position in Petrobras only to see it decline by 75 percent at one point in time. We also got caught in the newly developing petrochemical industry in the Gulf States.

Another instance where I failed to properly exploit a correct insight was in regard to the commodity bubble. I did recognize that the flight from currencies was turning a long-term uptrend in commodities into a bubble, and I so testified before Congress (see appendix). We did get out of our strategic long position in CVRD, the Brazilian iron ore producer, in time and shorted other major iron ore producers, but we missed a major opportunity in the commodities themselves—partly because I knew from past experience how difficult it is to trade them.

I was also slow to recognize the trend reversal in the dollar and gave back a large portion of our profits. Under the direction of my new Chief Investment Officer, we did make money in the United Kingdom, where we bet that short-term interest rates would decline and shorted sterling versus the euro. We also made good money by going long the credit markets in the United States after their collapse.

Eventually I understood that the strength of the dollar was due not to people choosing to hold dollars but to their inability to maintain or roll over their dollar obligations. In a very real sense, the strength of the dollar, like the fever associated with sickness, was a measure of the disruption of the financial system. This insight helped me to anticipate the downturn of the dollar at the end of 2008. As a result, we ended the year modestly higher, almost meeting my target of 10 percent annual minimum return, after spending most of the year in the red. I consider this quite an accomplishment in a period of almost universal wealth destruction.

THE CRASH OF 2008

The bankruptcy of Lehman Brothers on Monday, September 15, 2008, was a game-changing event. As I have noted, until then, whenever the financial system came close to a breakdown, the authorities intervened. This time they did not. The consequences were disastrous. CDSs (credit default swaps) went through the roof, and American International Group (AIG), which carried a large short position in CDSs, was facing imminent default. By the next day, Tuesday, Treasury Secretary Henry Paulson had to reverse himself and come to the rescue of AIG, albeit on extremely punitive terms. But worse was to come. Lehman was one of the main market-makers in commercial paper and a major issuer. An independent money market fund held Lehman paper, and, since it had no deep pocket to turn to, it had to "break the buck"—stop redeeming its shares at par. This caused panic among depositors, and by Thursday a run on money market funds was in full swing. The panic spread to the stock market. The Federal Reserve had to extend a guarantee to all money market funds, short selling of financial stocks was suspended, and the Treasury announced a $700 billion rescue package for the banking system. This provided some temporary relief to the stock market.

Paulson's $700 billion rescue package was ill conceived; more exactly, it was not conceived at all. Strange as it is, the Treasury Secretary was simply not prepared for the consequences of his action when he allowed Lehman Brothers to fail. When the financial system collapsed, he had to rush to Congress without any clear idea of how he was going to use the money he was asking for, and only a rudimentary concept of setting up something like the Resolution Trust Corporation, which acquired and eventually disposed of the assets of failing savings and loan institutions in the savings and loan crisis of the 1980s. So he asked for total discretion, including immunity from legal challenge. Unsurprisingly, Congress did not give it to him. Several voices, my own included, argued convincingly that the money would be better spent injecting equity into banks rather than taking toxic assets off their hands. Eventually Secretary Paulson came around to the idea but did not execute it properly. I outlined how it should have been done in two articles, which are included in the appendix.

Conditions in the financial system continued to deteriorate. The commercial paper market ground to a halt, LIBOR rose, swap spreads widened, CDSs blew out, and investment banks and other financial institutions without direct access to the Federal Reserve could not get access to overnight or short-term credit. The Fed had to extend one lifeline after another. It was in this atmosphere that the International Monetary Fund (IMF) held its annual meeting in Washington, starting on October 11, 2008. The European leaders left early and met in Paris on Sunday, October 12. At that meeting they decided to guarantee, in effect, that no major European financial institution would be allowed to fail. They could not agree, however, to do it on an inclusive Europe-wide basis, so each country set up its own arrangements. The United States followed suit in short order.

These arrangements had an unintended adverse side effect: They brought additional pressure to bear on the countries that could not extend similarly credible guarantees to their financial institutions. Iceland was already in a state of collapse. The largest bank in Hungary was now subjected to a bear raid, and the currencies and government bond markets of Hungary and the other Eastern European countries fell precipitously. The same happened to Brazil, Mexico, the Asian tigers, and to a lesser extent Turkey, South Africa, China, India, Australia, and New Zealand. The euro tanked and the yen soared. The dollar strengthened on a trade-weighted basis. Trade credit in the periphery countries dried up. The precipitous currency moves claimed some victims. Leading exporters in Brazil had gotten into the habit of selling options against their appreciating currency and now became insolvent, precipitating a local mini-crash.

All these dislocations taken together had a tremendous impact on the behavior and attitudes of consumers, businesses, and financial institutions throughout the world. The financial system had been in crisis since August 2007, but the general public hardly noticed it and, with some exceptions, business carried on as usual. All this changed in the weeks following September 15, 2008. The global economy fell off a cliff, and this became evident as the statistics for October and November began to appear. The wealth effect was enormous. Pension funds, university endowments, and charitable institutions lost anywhere between 20 and 40 percent of their assets within a couple of months—and that was before the $50 billion Bernard Madoff scandal was exposed. The self-reinforcing recognition that we are facing a deep and long recession, possibly amounting to a depression, has become widespread.

The Federal Reserve responded forcefully, slashing the Fed fund rate to practically zero on December 16, 2008, and embarking on quantitative easing. The Obama administration is preparing a two-year fiscal stimulus package in the $850 billion range and other radical measures.

The international response has been more muted. The IMF has approved a new facility that allows periphery countries in sound financial condition to borrow up to five times their quota without conditionality, but the amounts are puny and the possibility of a stigma continues to linger. As a result, the facility remains unused. The Fed opened swap lines with Mexico, Brazil, Korea, and Singapore. But European Central Bank President Jean-Claude Trichet inveighed against fiscal irresponsibility, and Germany remains adamantly opposed to excessive money creation that may lay the groundwork for inflationary pressures in the future. These divergent attitudes render concerted international action extremely difficult to achieve. They may also cause wide swings in exchange rates.

In retrospect, the bankruptcy of Lehman Brothers is comparable to the bank failures that occurred in the 1930s. How could it have been allowed to occur? The responsibility lies squarely with the financial authorities, notably the Treasury and the Federal Reserve. They claim that they lacked the necessary legal powers, but that is a lame excuse. In an emergency they could and should have done whatever was necessary to prevent the system from collapsing. That is what they have done on other occasions. The fact is, they allowed it to happen. Why?

I would draw a distinction between Treasury Secretary Henry Paulson and Federal Reserve Chairman Ben Bernanke. Paulson was in charge because Lehman Brothers, as an investment bank, was not under the aegis of the Federal

Reserve. In my view, Paulson was reluctant to resort to the use of "taxpayers' money" because he knew that it would entail increased government control. He was a true market fundamentalist. He believed that the same methods and instruments that got the markets into trouble could be used to get them out of it. This led to his abortive plan to create a super-SIV (Special Investment Vehicle) to take over failing SIVs. He subscribed to the doctrine that markets have greater powers to adjust than any individual participant. Coming six months after the Bear Stearns crisis, he must have thought that markets had had enough notice to prepare for the failure of Lehman Brothers. That is why he had no Plan B when the markets broke down.

Ben Bernanke was less of an ideologue. But coming from an academic background, the bursting of the super-bubble found him unprepared. He asserted that the housing bubble was an isolated phenomenon that could cause losses up to $100 billion, which could be easily absorbed. He did not realize that equilibrium theory was fundamentally flawed; as a consequence, he could not anticipate that the various methods and instruments based on the false assumption that prices deviate from a theoretical equilibrium in a random manner would fail one after another in short order. But he was a fast learner. When he saw it happening he responded by drastically lowering interest rates, first in January 2008 and again in December. Unfortunately, his learning process started too late and always lagged behind the actual course of events. That is how the situation spun out of control.

On a deeper level, the demise of Lehman Brothers conclusively falsifies the efficient market hypothesis. My argument is bound to be controversial, but it raises some very interesting questions. Each of its three steps will take the reader to unfamiliar grounds.

The first step is to acknowledge that there is an asymmetry between being long or short in the stock market. (Being long means owning a stock; being short means selling a stock one does not own). As discussed earlier, going long has unlimited potential on the upside, but limited exposure on the downside. Being short is the reverse. The asymmetry manifests itself in the following way: Losing on a long position reduces one's risk exposure while losing on a short position increases it. As a result, one can be more patient being long and wrong than being short and wrong. The asymmetry serves to discourage the short-selling of stocks.

The second step is to understand CDSs and to recognize that the CDS market offers a convenient way of shorting bonds. In that market the risk-reward asymmetry works in the opposite way to stocks. Going short bonds by buying a CDS contract carries limited risk but unlimited profit potential; by contrast, selling CDSs offers limited profits but practically unlimited risks. The asymmetry encourages speculating on the short side, which in turn exerts a downward pressure on the underlying bonds. When an adverse development is expected, the negative effect can become overwhelming because CDSs tend to be priced as warrants, not as options: People buy them not because they expect an eventual default but because they expect the CDS to appreciate in case of adverse developments. No arbitrage can correct the mispricing. That can be clearly seen in the case of U.S. and U.K. government bonds: The actual price of the bonds is much higher than the price implied by CDSs.

These asymmetries are difficult to reconcile with the efficient market hypothesis.

The third step is to take into account reflexivity and recognize that the mispricing of financial instruments can affect the fundamentals that market prices are supposed to reflect. Nowhere is this phenomenon more pronounced than in the case of financial institutions whose ability to do business is so dependent on confidence and trust. A decline in their share and bond prices can increase their financing costs. That means that bear raids on financial institutions can be self-validating, which is in direct contradiction of the efficient market hypothesis.

Putting these three considerations together leads to the conclusion that Lehman Brothers, AIG, and other financial institutions were destroyed by bear raids in which the shorting of stocks and buying of CDSs mutually amplified and reinforced each other. The unlimited shorting of stocks was made possible by the abolition of the uptick rule (which would have hindered bear raids by allowing short selling only when prices were rising). The unlimited shorting of bonds was facilitated by the CDS market. The two together made a lethal combination. That is what AIG, one of the most successful insurance companies in the world, failed to understand. Its business was selling insurance, and when it saw a seriously mispriced risk it went to town insuring it in the belief that diversifying risk reduces it. It expected to make a fortune in the long run, but it was destroyed in the short run because it did not realize that it was selling not insurance but warrants for shorting bonds.

My argument lends itself to empirical research. The evidence shows that the CDS market is much larger than all the bond markets put together—having peaked at an amazing $62 trillion nominal amount outstanding. There is only anecdotal evidence that there was some collusion between the people who shorted stocks and bought CDSs, but the matter could be further investigated. The *prima facie* evidence favors the conclusion.

This raises some interesting questions. What would have happened if the uptick rule had been kept in effect and speculating in CDSs had been outlawed? The bankruptcy of Lehman Brothers might have been avoided, but what would have happened to the super-bubble? One can only conjecture. My guess is that the super-bubble would have been deflated more slowly, with less catastrophic results, but the aftereffects would have lingered longer. It would have resembled the Japanese experience more than what is happening now.

What is the proper role of short selling? Undoubtedly it gives markets greater depth and continuity, making them more resilient, but it is not without dangers. Bear raids can be self-validating and ought to be kept under control. If the efficient market hypothesis were valid, there would be an *a priori* reason for imposing no constraints. As it is, both the uptick rule and allowing short selling only when it is covered by actually borrowed stock are useful pragmatic measures that seem to work well without any clear-cut theoretical justification.

What about credit default swaps? Here I take a more radical view than most people. The prevailing view is that they ought to be traded on regulated exchanges. I believe they are toxic and should be used only by prescription. They could be allowed to be used to insure actual bonds but—in light of their asymmetric character—not to speculate against countries or companies.* CDSs are not the only synthetic financial instruments that have proven toxic. The same applies to the slicing and dicing of CDOs (collateralized debt obligations) and to the portfolio insurance contracts that caused the stock market crash of 1987, to mention only two that have actually done a lot of damage. The issuance of stock is closely regulated by the SEC; why not the issuance of derivatives and other synthetic instruments? The role of reflexivity and the asymmetries I have identified ought to prompt a rejection of the efficient market hypothesis and a thorough reconsideration of the regulatory regime.

Now that the bankruptcy of Lehman Brothers has had the same shock effect on the behavior of consumers and businesses as the bank failures of the 1930s, the problems facing the Obama administration are at least twice as great as those that confronted President Roosevelt. This can be seen from a simple calculation. Total credit outstanding was 160 percent of GDP in 1929, and it rose to 260 percent in 1932 due to the accumulation of debt and the decline of GDP. We entered into the Crash of 2008 at 365 percent, which is bound to rise to 500 percent or more by the time the full effect is felt. And this calculation does not take into account the pervasive use of derivatives, which was absent in the 1930s but immensely complicates the current situation.

---

*Early in 2009, trading in CDSs is creating trouble for the euro. Several countries within the Euroblock are getting over-indebted and facing the prospect of being downgraded by the rating agencies. The buying of CDS contracts puts additional pressure on their borrowing costs and diminishes the benefit of being members of the euroblock. This casts doubts on the durability of the euro. There is an independently existing underlying weakness in the euro, which is exacerbated by the CDS market in a self-reinforcing fashion.

The nominal amount of CDS contracts outstanding is more than four times the GDP. On the positive side, we have the experience of the 1930s and the prescriptions of John Maynard Keynes to draw on. His *The General Theory of Employment, Interest, and Money* was published only in 1936; we have it at our disposal from the outset. Drawing on it, let me first outline the policies that the Obama administration ought to pursue, and then assess how the future may play out.

10

An Economic Recovery Program

The bursting of bubbles causes credit contraction, forced liquidation of assets, deflation, and wealth destruction that may reach catastrophic proportions. In a deflationary environment, the weight of accumulated debt can sink the banking system and push the economy into depression. That is what needs to be prevented at all costs.

It can be done by creating money to offset the contraction of credit, recapitalizing the banking system, and writing off or down the accumulated debt in an orderly manner. For best results, the three processes should be combined. This requires radical and unorthodox policy measures. If these measures were successful and credit started to expand, deflationary pressures would be replaced by the specter of inflation, and the authorities would have to drain the excess money supply from the economy almost as fast as they pumped it in. Of the two operations, the second is likely to prove both technically and politically even more difficult than the first, but the alternative—global depression and world disorder—is unacceptable. There is no way to escape from a far-from-equilibrium situation—global deflation and depression—except by first inducing its opposite and then reducing it.

As we have seen, the size of the problem is even larger than it was in the 1930s. The situation has been further aggravated by the haphazard and arbitrary way in which it was handled by the Bush administration. The public and the business community suffered a shock in the aftermath of the Lehman Brothers default, and the economy has fallen off a cliff. The next two quarters will show rapid deterioration.

To prevent the economy from sliding into a depression, President Obama must embark on a radical and comprehensive policy package that has five major components:

1. A fiscal stimulus package
2. A thorough overhaul of the mortgage system
3. Recapitalization of the banking system
4. An innovative energy policy
5. Reform of the international financial system

I shall briefly discuss each of these elements.

1. A Fiscal Stimulus Package

This is conventional wisdom, and I have nothing original to contribute. The fiscal stimulus package is already well advanced, and it will be the first out of the gate, but it will take time to implement and will serve merely to moderate the downturn. In my view the next two items are indispensable. To turn the economy around, the mortgage and banking systems need to be thoroughly reorganized and restarted.

2. A Thorough Overhaul of the Mortgage System

The collapse of the financial system started with the bursting of the U.S. housing bubble. There is a real danger now that house prices will overshoot on the downside and put further pressure on the banks' balance sheets. To prevent this, foreclosures must be reduced to a minimum and house ownership facilitated both for new buyers and current owners. But we ought to go even further than that. With the mortgage financing industry in shambles, we ought to subject it to a thorough overhaul and introduce a new system that is free of the deficiencies that are responsible for our current difficulties. It is rare that a systemic change is necessary or even possible; the present is such an occasion.

I advocate adopting, with suitable modifications, the Danish system, which has proven its worth since it was first introduced after the Great Fire of Copenhagen in 1795. Our current system has broken down because the originators of mortgages have not retained any part of the credit risk. They are motivated to maximize their fee income. As agents, their interests are not identical with the interests of the ultimate owners. In the Danish system, the service companies retain the credit risk—they have to replace the mortgages that are in default.

In contrast to our reliance on government sponsored enterprises (GSEs)—namely Fannie Mae and Freddie Mac—the Danish is an open system in which all mortgage originators participate on equal terms, and it operates without government guarantees. Yet Danish mortgage bonds are traditionally very highly rated; often they yield less than government bonds. This could not be replicated in the United States at present because of the demoralized state of the market, but it may be achieved later.

Danish mortgage bonds are highly standardized, and their distinguishing feature is that they are identical to and interchangeable with the underlying mortgages. House owners can redeem their mortgages at any time by purchasing the equivalent mortgage bond in the market and exchanging it for the mortgage. Since bond prices and house prices normally move in the same direction, this feature—called the principle of balance—reduces the chances of householders having negative equity in their houses. The mortgage originators are strictly regulated, and their interests are closely aligned with those of the bondholders. They pass on only the interest rate risk to bondholders, retaining the credit risk. That is why the bonds are so highly rated.

When Mexico wanted to securitize mortgages in order to promote house ownership, it opted, with my assistance, for the Danish system. My proposal was supported by the U.S. Treasury, which was then under the leadership of Paul O'Neill. The Danish model is clearly superior to the GSE model. The question is, how can you get there from here?

Originally, I proposed a grand scheme in which *all* mortgages that are under water (i.e., whose principal amount exceeds the current market value of the house) would be replaced by a new mortgage, incorporating the Danish principle of balance but being insured by a government agency. This would have had the advantage of removing the incentive to default in order to obtain the benefits of loan modification, but it would have run into insuperable political and even constitutional difficulties. The slicing and dicing of CDOs has created such conflicts of interest amongst the holders of various tranches that neither a voluntary nor a compulsory scheme of reorganization is possible.

Abandoning the search for an optimal solution, I have come to realize that a second best solution is readily available. The GSEs have become effectively government owned, but the government is not exercising its powers of control. They are in limbo, torn between the interests of their shareholders and the public. The prospect of the shareholders emerging with a positive value is imaginary; nevertheless, the GSEs are trying to make a profit from their quasi-monopolistic position, charging heavy fees and imposing restrictive conditions on both refinancing applications and new ones. This is aggravating the housing problem, but it could easily be changed by a newly established regulator asserting its authority and using the GSEs as an instrument of public policy.

The GSEs could then introduce a new type of mortgage contract based on the Danish model. It would be transparent and uniform, and it would incorporate the principle of balance. The GSEs would reduce their fees, extend the limit on the size of mortgages they are willing to guarantee, and introduce a new line of guarantees—up to 90 percent of appraised value at a higher premium—effectively replacing the private mortgage insurance companies that have become inactive. They would then introduce a streamlined and cheap refinancing process for existing mortgages. That would greatly reduce the cost of conforming mortgages and create a powerful incentive to convert nonconforming mortgages into conforming ones. Owners of defaulting mortgages could avail themselves of the provisions of the Help for Homeowners Act and realize 85 percent of the appraised value. In most cases this would be preferable to going through a costly foreclosure process. If owners failed to choose that route, it could be imposed on them by a judge in a simplified bankruptcy process. One way or another, the number of foreclosures would be greatly reduced, and with mortgages more freely available at lower cost, house prices would stabilize at a higher level than would otherwise be the case. Financial institutions would recover some of their losses on residential mortgages and securities.

It is ironic that the GSEs, which are at the root of the problem, should provide a route to the solution. In the long run the GSEs should be phased out and their portfolios run off. They would become a government agency in charge of mortgage guarantees issued by the government. Eventually, when the modified Danish model becomes firmly established, even that function could be phased out. Under the new system, mortgage origination companies would remain responsible for the first 10 percent of any losses arising out of default. They would be allowed to charge a fee that would be determined by competition. As the system matures, service companies may find it advantageous to accept the entire credit risk and not pay a fee for government guarantees. The system would then come to reflect the Danish model more faithfully.

The sequence of the GSEs first becoming more important and then fading away resembles the sequence that characterizes the entire process—to escape deflation you first induce inflation and then reduce it. In implementing it we should never forget what went wrong with communism: the state did not fade away. The fading away should be part of the plan from inception.

The whole process could be accomplished by using the GSEs and the new bankruptcy law currently under consideration by Congress. The government already controls the GSEs; all it has to do is to exercise its powers. The cramdown provisions of the proposed new bankruptcy law face active opposition from many financial institutions holding mortgages; it should be possible to persuade them that most of them would benefit from the mortgage reorganization scheme outlined here. The costs to the taxpayers would manifest themselves through the eventual losses incurred by the GSEs, but, considering the impact on house prices and the economy, the net effect is likely to be positive.

3. RECAPITALIZATION OF THE BANKING SYSTEM

I cannot present as clear a picture of what a reformed banking system would look like as I can for the mortgage system because there are no suitable models to invoke. The Spanish banking system has weathered a bigger boom in house construction better than the U.S. banking system, and it has some desirable features, but Spain is even more adversely affected by the Crash of 2008 than the United States. What happened to the U.S. banking system after the Great Depression certainly does not present a desirable model. Banks were put into a straightjacket whose constraints began to be loosened only in the 1970s. We are in uncharted territory.

I summed up the main lessons to be learned from the current financial crisis in the previous edition of this book: Financial markets do not tend toward equilibrium, and deviations are not random. Credit creation and contraction are reflexive and tend to occur in initially self-reinforcing but eventually self-defeating boom-bust sequences. Therefore it is not enough to regulate the money supply; it is also necessary to regulate credit conditions. This involves reactivating policy tools that have fallen into disuse: variable margin and minimum capital requirements, and central bank directives on bank lending to particular sectors. Not only banks but all institutions involved in credit creation must be subject to regulation. The objective is to maintain stability and prevent mispricing and other excesses from becoming self-reinforcing. The same applies to financial instruments: They need to be licensed and supervised to ensure that they are uniform and transparent and do not destabilize markets. Leverage must be used cautiously: It is not enough to allow for quantifiable risks; one must impose an additional safety margin for the uncertainties inherent in reflexivity. Financial engineering, structured finance, and other innovations are of dubious value; insofar as they circumvent regulations or render them ineffective, they can be harmful.

It is clear, in the light of these observations, that the financial sector became far too big and profitable. In the future it will have to shrink and remain within the control of the authorities. While financial markets became global, the authorities remained national. Since global markets are beneficial, the authorities must also become more international and the international financial institutions must serve the interests of all their members more equitably.

Since the publication of the previous edition of this book, financial markets have completely collapsed and had to be put on artificial life support. Keeping them alive and preventing the world economy from sliding into depression has to take precedence over all other considerations. As we have seen, the economy can be turned around only in two steps. The first is to offset the collapse of credit by creating money, writing off bad debt, and recapitalizing the banks. Then, if and when that succeeds, the excess money supply will have to be drained as fast as credit begins to flow. That means the initial policy measures will take us in exactly the opposite direction from our eventual destination. Nevertheless, the ultimate destination ought to inform the design of the initial step. Unfortunately, Treasury Secretary Henry Paulson reacted in a haphazard and capricious manner. That is how the situation spun out of control. After the bankruptcy of Lehman Brothers, he forced through Congress a $700 billion rescue package without any clear idea how it should be used to adequately recapitalize the banks. I explained how it should be done in an article published by the *Financial Times* online on October 1, 2008, at the height of the Congressional debate. This is what I proposed:

The Treasury secretary would give bank examiners clear guidelines for how assets should be valued. For instance, it would be postulated that commercial real estate will on average lose 30 percent of its value. He would then ask the examiners to establish how much additional equity capital each bank needs in order to be properly capitalized according to existing capital requirements. If managements could not raise equity from the private sector, they could turn to the Treasury. The Treasury would offer to underwrite an issue of convertible preference shares. The preference shares would carry a low coupon (say 5 percent) so that banks would find it profitable to continue lending, but shareholders would be heavily diluted by the convertibility feature. They would be given the right, however, to subscribe on the Treasury's terms, and if they exercised their rights, they would avoid dilution. The rights would be tradeable, and the Treasury would seek to set the terms so that the rights would have a positive value. Private investors, including me, may be interested in buying the shares of some banks on the same terms as the Treasury.

After recapitalization, minimum capital requirements would be lowered to, say, 6 percent. This would encourage banks to lend because they could suffer a further 25 percent depreciation of assets without violating statutory limits. They would be eager to take advantage of the rich margins currently prevailing. The economy would be reactivated. With everyone sitting on a lot of liquidity and suddenly eager to put it to work, there would be a sudden rush into less liquid assets. Deflation would be replaced by the specter of inflation, and liquidity would have to be drained as fast as it had been pumped in. Minimum capital requirements would then be raised first to 8 percent, then higher. In this way, the leverage of the banking system would be reduced, which is a desirable long-term objective.

If TARP (the Troubled Asset Relief Program) had been implemented in this way originally, the banking system could have been recapitalized with $700 billion, or perhaps even less. Unfortunately, half that money has already been spent, and most of the second half of TARP will also be needed to plug the holes that have already developed. What would have been possible then is no longer realistic. That is a distinguishing feature of financial crises and other far-from-equilibrium conditions: What is appropriate at one point in time is no longer valid at the next one.

Adequate recapitalization of the banking system now faces two seemingly insuperable obstacles. One is that Treasury Secretary Henry Paulson has poisoned the well by the arbitrary and ill-considered way he forced through and implemented the $700 billion TARP program. The Obama administration feels that it cannot ask Congress for more money. The other is that the hole in the banks' balance sheets has become much bigger since TARP was introduced. The assets of the banks—real estate, securities, and consumer and commercial loans—have continued to deteriorate, and the market value of banks' stocks has continued to decline. It is estimated that something in the neighborhood of an additional trillion-and-a-half dollars would be required to adequately recapitalize the banks. Since their total market capitalization has fallen to about a trillion dollars, this raises the specter of nationalization, which is politically—and even culturally—unpalatable.

Consequently, the administration is constrained to do what is possible even if it falls short of what is necessary. It plans to carve out up to $100 billion from the second tranche of TARP in order to set up an aggregator bank that would acquire toxic assets from the banks' balance sheets. By obtaining 10:1 leverage from the balance sheet of the Federal Reserve, the aggregator bank could have a trillion dollars at its disposal. That is not sufficient to cleanse the balance sheets of the banks and restart lending, but it would bring some welcome relief. The aggregator bank could serve as a useful interim measure except for the fact that it is liable to make it more difficult to obtain funding necessary for a proper recapitalization in the future. It will encounter all kinds of difficulties in valuing toxic securities and even if these could be overcome it will still end up as a covert subsidy to the banks by bidding up the price of their toxic assets. There will be tremendous political resistance to any further expenditure to bail out the banks. This will make it much more difficult to mobilize additional funds in the future. It would be a pity to take the aggregator bank route, especially when there is a way to adequately recapitalize the banks with the currently available resources.

Let me spell out how it could be done. The trick is not to remove the toxic assets from the balance sheets of the banks but to put them into a "side pocket" or "sidecar" as hedge funds are now doing with their illiquid assets. The appropriate amount of capital—equity and subordinated debt—would be sequestered in the side pocket. This would cleanse the balance sheets and create good banks, but leave them undercapitalized. The same trillion dollars that is currently destined to fund the aggregator bank could then be used to infuse capital into the good banks. Although the hole is bigger, a trillion dollars would be more than sufficient because it would be possible to mobilize significant amounts from the private sector.

In the current environment a good bank would enjoy exceptionally good margins. Margins would narrow as a result of competition but by then the banking system would be revitalized and nationalization avoided. The situation is analogous to a devastating hurricane depleting the capital of property insurance companies, raising insurance premiums, and attracting additional capital into the industry.

The scheme I am proposing would minimize valuation problems and avoid providing a hidden subsidy to the banks. Exactly for that reason it is likely to encounter strong resistance from vested interests. Losses would first accrue to shareholders and debenture holders; only if they exceed a bank's capital would the FDIC be liable for the deficiency, as it is already. Shareholders would be severely diluted, but they would be given tradable rights to subscribe to the good bank, and if there is a positive residue in the side pocket, it would also revert to the good bank as of the date of the new issue, giving shareholders the benefit of any subsequent appreciation. The fact that debenture holders may lose money will make it more difficult to sell bank debentures in the future. But that is as it should be: Banks should not be as highly leveraged as they have recently been. Pension funds would suffer heavy losses; but that is preferable to taxpayers taking over those losses.

In addition to restarting bank lending, my scheme would resolve the moral hazard issue for a long time to come. The banking industry is accustomed to turning to the state in a crisis and effectively demanding a bailout on the grounds that financial capital has to be protected to ensure the proper functioning of the economy. Given the aversion to state ownership of banks, the blackmail has always worked. That is how the bubble grew so large. The Obama administration ought to resist the blackmail and adopt the scheme outlined here as a prelude to building a better financial system. Our future depends on it.

4. An Innovative Energy Policy

Energy policy could play a much more innovative role in counteracting both recession and deflation. The American consumer can no longer act as the motor of the global economy. A new motor is needed. Alternative energies and energy savings could serve as that motor, but only if the price of conventional fuels is kept high enough to justify investing in them. That might also help to moderate price deflation. A high price on conventional fuels would be beneficial on both counts, but it would be hard to sell to the public. Until now, no politician dared to do so.

President Obama would need great courage and great skill to do the right thing. This would involve putting a floor under the price of fossil fuels by

1. imposing a price on carbon emissions by (a) a carbon tax or (b) auctioning pollution licenses (the former would be more efficient, the latter is politically more acceptable) and

2. imposing import duties on oil to keep the domestic price above, say, $70 per barrel.

The anticipated income from carbon emissions should then be distributed to households in full and in advance. This would compensate them for the higher cost of energy and hopefully make the scheme politically acceptable. It would also act as a temporary fiscal stimulus at a time when it is most needed, although most of it can be expected to be saved rather than spent. Gradually the price of carbon emissions would have to be raised to a level where it would pay to remove carbon from coal. This is indispensable for bringing climate change under control because there is no adequate substitute for coal-fired power plants except clean coal.

It is essential to convince the public that the cost of energy will remain high for some time in order to encourage investment in alternative energy and energy-saving devices. Eventually the cost of energy may decline as new technologies travel down the learning curve. We cannot depend on the price mechanism alone to ensure the development of new technologies. Tax concessions, subsidies, vehicle emissions standards, and building codes are also needed. Even so, neither energy security nor the control of global warming can be achieved without putting a price on carbon emissions. The United States cannot do it alone, but it cannot be done without the United States taking the lead.

5. REFORM OF THE INTERNATIONAL FINANCIAL SYSTEM

The fate of the United States is intimately interconnected with the rest of the world. The international financial system as it has evolved since the 1980s has been dominated by the United States and the Washington consensus. Far from providing a level playing field, it has favored the United States, to the detriment of the countries at the periphery. The United States exercises veto rights over the international financial institutions (IFIs)—the International Monetary Fund (IMF) and the World Bank. The periphery countries are subject to the market discipline dictated by the Washington consensus, but the United States is exempt from it. This has exposed the periphery countries to a series of financial crises and forced them to follow pro-cyclical fiscal policies, and it has allowed the United States to suck up the savings of the rest of the world and maintain an ever-increasing current account deficit. This trend might have continued indefinitely because the willingness of the United States to run a chronic current account deficit was matched by the willingness of other countries to run current account surpluses. It was brought to an end by the bursting of the housing bubble, which exposed the overindebtedness of the household sector.

The current financial crisis has revealed how unfair the system is because it originated in the United States, but it is doing more damage to the periphery than to the center. This damage to the periphery is a recent development, following the bankruptcy of Lehman Brothers, and its significance has not yet been fully recognized. The countries at the center have effectively guaranteed their bank deposits, but the periphery countries cannot offer similarly convincing guarantees. As a result, capital is fleeing the periphery, and it is difficult to roll over maturing loans. Exports suffer for the lack of trade finance.

The IFIs are now faced with a novel task: to protect the countries of the periphery from a storm that has emanated from the center, namely the United States. The IFIs' future depends on how well they cope with that task. Unless they can provide significant assistance, they may become largely irrelevant. Global, multilateral arrangements are in danger of breaking down, turning the financial crisis into global disorder and depression.

Assistance is needed to

- protect the financial systems of periphery countries, including trade finance, and
- enable periphery governments to engage in countercyclical fiscal policies.

The former requires large contingency funds available at short notice for relatively short periods of time. The latter requires long-term financing.

When the adverse side effects of the Lehman bankruptcy on the periphery countries became evident, the IMF introduced a new short-term liquidity (STL) facility that allows countries that are otherwise in sound financial condition to borrow five times their quota for three months without any conditionality. But the size of the STL is too small to be of much use, especially while a potential stigma associated with the use of IMF funds lingers. Even if it worked, any help for the top-tier countries would merely aggravate the situation of the lower-tier countries. International assistance to enable periphery countries to engage in countercyclical policies has not even been considered.

The fact is that the IMF simply does not have enough money to offer meaningful relief. It has about $200 billion in uncommitted funds at its disposal, and the potential needs are much greater. What is to be done? The simplest solution is to create more money. The mechanism for issuing Special Drawing Rights (SDRs) already exists. All it takes to activate it is the approval of 85 percent of the membership. In the past the United States has been the holdout opposing it. Creating additional money supply is the right response to the collapse of credit. That is what the United States is doing domestically. Why not do it internationally?

Ironically, SDR would not be of much use in providing short-term liquidity, but it would be very helpful in enabling periphery countries to engage in countercyclical policies. This would be done by rich countries lending or, preferably, *donating* their allocations to poor countries. The scheme has the merit that the IFIs would retain control over the disbursement of the lent or donated funds and ensure that they are spent in accordance with the poverty reduction programs that have already been prepared at the behest of the World Bank. This would especially benefit poorer countries that are liable to be hardest hit by the worldwide recession.

If it were implemented on a large scale—say $1 trillion—the SDR scheme could make a major contribution to both fighting the global recession and fulfilling the United Nations' Millennium Development Goals. This seemingly selfless act by rich countries would actually serve their enlightened self-interests because it would not only help turn around the global economy but also reinforce the market for their export industries.

Since the SDR scheme is not of much use in providing short-term liquidity to periphery countries, that task would have to be accomplished by other means, notably the following three:

1. Chronic surplus countries could contribute to a trust fund that supplements the new STL facility. This would greatly enhance the value of that facility by removing the five-times-quota limitation. For instance, under STL Brazil can draw only $23.4 billion, while its own reserves are over

$200 billion. A more flexible supplemental fund would give the STL facility more heft. Japan held out the promise of $100 billion. Other chronic surplus countries probably would not contribute unless the quota issue was reopened. Holding out the prospect of higher quotas could serve as an inducement to put together a supplemental fund that would be large enough to be convincing.

2. The central banks of the developed world should extend additional swap lines to developing countries, and they should accept assets denominated in local currencies to make them more effective. The IMF could play a role by guaranteeing the value of assets denominated in local currencies.

3. In the longer term, international banking regulations should facilitate credit flows to periphery countries. In the short term, the central banks of the developed countries should exert pressure on commercial banks under their aegis to roll over credit lines. This could be perhaps coordinated by the Bank for International Settlements.

With regard to enabling periphery countries to engage in countercyclical policies:

1. The major developed countries should, in addition to donating their SDR allocations, jointly guarantee, within agreed limits, longer-term government bond issues of periphery countries. Regional arrangements should be encouraged, provided they are within an international framework. For instance, the European Investment Bank and the European Bank for Reconstruction and Development should finance public works in Ukraine in conjunction with the IMF package. China's interest in Africa and other raw material–producing

areas should be encouraged, provided China observes the Extractive Industries Transparency Initiative and other international standards.

2. The chronic surplus countries could be induced, by offering them additional voting rights, to invest a portion of their currency reserves or sovereign wealth funds in longer-term government bonds of less developed countries. This could be connected with the proposed trust fund supplementing the STL facility.

None of these measures is possible without opening up the vexed question of quota redistribution. This would be in the enlightened self-interest of both the United States and the European countries that would give up some of their voting rights, because in its absence the newly rich countries would have no interest in cooperating with the IMF. They would turn to bilateral or regional arrangements, and the IMF would become largely irrelevant. The question probably cannot be avoided anyhow, but it will take a long time to settle. The best course would be to obtain support for a large-scale SDR scheme by agreeing to open negotiations. President Obama would be fulfilling the world's expectations by championing this course. The main opposition is likely to come from Germany, but with U.S. leadership and broad international support it could be overcome.

In addition, many other international arrangements are needed:

- Banking regulations need to be internationally coordinated. This would be the task of a Basel Three accord. (Basel Two has been discredited by the financial crisis.)

- Market regulations also need to be global.
- National governments need to coordinate their macro-economic policies in order to avoid wide currency swings and other disruptions.
- Commodity stabilization schemes ought to be considered. They could be particularly helpful for commodity-dependent periphery countries and in counteracting the prevailing worldwide deflationary tendencies.

This is a condensed, almost shorthand, account of what needs to be done to turn the global economy around. It should give a sense of how difficult a task it is. It remains to be seen whether any of ideas laid out here are adopted as policy.

CHAPTER 11

My Outlook for 2009

The future of the global economy will greatly depend on whether President Obama embarks on a comprehensive and coherent set of measures such as those I have outlined here. How the Chinese, the Europeans, and other major players respond will be almost as important. If there is good international cooperation, the world economy may start climbing out of a deep hole by the end of 2009. In the absence of a coordinated approach, we are headed for economic and political disorder and decline of much longer duration. Even with the best cooperation, we are liable to experience some rather wild market swings.

There is no way to reestablish equilibrium in one fell swoop. The process has to go through at least two stages: First, the economy has to be pumped full of money to make up for the collapse of credit; then, when credit begins to flow again, the liquidity has to be drained out of the system almost as fast as it was injected. As I mentioned before, the second operation will be both politically and technically more difficult than the first: Congress finds it much easier to give money away than to impose taxes. It is all the more important that stimulus packages should be channeled into relatively productive investments. The bailout of the motor industry ought to be the exception, not the rule.

The Agency Problem

In the next two years, the government will play a disproportionately large role in the economy, because it will be almost the sole source of new financing. It will come to own a significant part of the banking system and, through the banks, a significant stake in commercial real estate. It will have a major say in the motor industry, but hopefully not in too many others. It will have a deep involvement in the residential housing market. This will give rise to a gigantic agency problem—the problem that arises when agents put their own interests ahead of the interests of their principals. The agency problem has been the undoing of socialism and communism. It would be a wonderful world if people contributed according to their abilities and received according to their needs, but in practice, those in charge tend to give precedence to their own and their loved ones' needs. Ironically, the agency problem has also been a major factor in the undoing of the housing market in the United States. When investment bankers repackaged mortgages in CDOs, they thought they were reducing risk through diversification; in fact they were creating risk by separating the interests of the agents from the interests of the owners.

The agency problem has no simple solution. Transparency and accountability help, but they are generalizations, and the devil is in the details. It is fortunate that an administration that did not believe in public service has just been replaced by one that does. President Obama has generated tremendous enthusiasm, and hopefully he will be able to convert it into a spirit of public service and identification with the public interest in a time of adversity. Even so, the government's outsized role presents a grave danger for the political and economic future of the country. I am reminded of Italy in the interwar period, which became fascist and ended up with state ownership of practically all heavy industry. State ownership of banks is preferable to a banking system that does not function, but the ownership should be designed to be temporary because the agency problem can only grow worse with the passage of time.

The recapitalization of the banking system and the reorganization of housing finance should be rules-based to the greatest extent possible. The monetary authorities—the Treasury and the Federal Reserve in particular—have developed a tradition of acting arbitrarily and secretly in crisis situations. This is necessary to prevent crises from getting out of control. But on Henry Paulson's watch the situation did get out of control, and his high-handed and capricious conduct made matters worse. Case-by-case decisions are vulnerable to lobbying and political influence. The Obama administration ought to establish a discontinuity by engaging in systemic reforms.

THE DOLLAR

The effort to pump the economy full of money will run into difficulties in two areas: exchange rates and interest rates. The dollar came under pressure early on in the current financial crisis, but it staged a strong recovery as the crisis worsened. As I belatedly realized, the strength of the dollar in the latter part of 2008 was due not to an increased desire to hold dollars but to increased difficulties in borrowing it. European and other international banks had acquired a lot of dollar-denominated assets, which they habitually funded in the interbank market; as the market dried up they were forced to buy dollars. At the same time, periphery countries also held a lot of dollar-denominated obligations, which they had to repay when they could not roll them over.

Russia and the East European countries on the periphery of the euro were tied much more to the euro. But when the Russian market collapsed, the effect on the dollar was the same, because the Russian central bank had overbought euros and had to sell them to defend the ruble.

The trend was temporarily reversed at the end of 2008 when the Federal Reserve lowered interest rates to practically zero and embarked on quantitative easing. The euro staged an explosive rally, but the rally was short-lived because the eurozone developed its own internal difficulties. Widespread riots in Greece drew attention to the plight of the southern-tier countries—Spain, Italy, and Greece—and of Ireland. CDS rates for these countries rose, their credit ratings were lowered, and the yield spreads on their government bonds versus Germany widened to an alarming extent. The euro headed lower from the very beginning of 2009, and even it was outpaced by sterling.

Going forward, the fact that Germany and the European Central Bank (ECB) hold a different view of the problem confronting the global economy than the rest of the world is liable to cause wide swings in exchange rates and hinder the recovery. The ECB operates under asymmetric guidelines: It is constitutionally obliged to be concerned only with maintaining price stability, not full employment; Germany still lives with the memory of the Weimar Republic's runaway inflation, which served as a prelude to the Nazi regime. Both considerations militate against fiscal irresponsibility and unlimited money creation. This should favor the euro as a store of value, but the internal tensions within Europe work in the opposite direction.

The fact that there is no Europewide mechanism for protecting the banking system means that each country has to act on its own, which raises doubts about their ability to do so. Is Ireland's credit good enough? Can the ECB accept the government debt of Greece as collateral beyond certain limits? The foundations of the Maastricht Treaty are shaking, and even the United Kingdom and Switzerland are facing grave difficulties in protecting their overgrown banks. As national regulators seek to protect their own banks, they may hurt the banking systems of other countries. For instance, Austrian and Italian banks are heavily exposed in Eastern Europe. The Royal Bank of Scotland, which is now majority owned by the British government, does the bulk of its business abroad; and a significant portion of housing in the United Kingdom is financed by foreign banks. Eventually, the various national authorities will have to protect each other, but it is only a common danger that will force them to do so.

The owners of wealth may increasingly turn to the yen and gold for safety, but they may run into resistance from the authorities—sooner in the case of the yen than gold. And there will be a tug-of-war between those who seek safety and those who need to use their reserves to save their businesses. With all these contradictory forces at work we can expect wild currency fluctuations.

Interest Rates

As noted, the way out of a deflationary trap is to first induce inflation and then to reduce it. That is an intricate operation and success is far from assured. As soon as economic activity in the United States revives, interest rates on government bonds are liable to shoot up; indeed, the yield curve is likely to steepen in anticipation. Either way, a rise in long-term interest rates is liable to choke off the recovery. The prospect of the greatly increased money supply turning into inflation is likely to lead to a period of stagflation. That, however, would be a high-class problem, a desirable outcome because it would avoid prolonged depression.

It is difficult, but not impossible, to imagine the U.S. economy growing at a rate of 3 percent or more in the decade ahead. The United States has been running a chronic current account deficit, which exceeded 6 percent of GDP at its peak. That will disappear, and it will leave behind a heavy burden of foreign debt that will be further swollen by the budget deficits of the next few years. Consumption as a share of GDP has to fall. The financial services sector, which has been the fastest growing segment of the economy, will shrink. With baby boomers retiring in increasing numbers, demographic trends have turned unfavorable. All these are negative influences.

What is to be expected on the positive side? More equitable income distribution, both domestically and internationally. Better social services, including education. A constructive energy policy leading to large-scale investments in alternative energy and energy saving. Reduced military expenditures. Faster growth in the developing world that provides better export markets and investment opportunities. But even with the best policies, domestic growth is liable to lag behind the global economy. If I had to choose from the various shapes that a recession can take, I would opt for an inverted square root sign ⎺⌄—, with the deepest point being reached around the end of 2009.

CHINA

The most important factor in the developing world is China. China has been the main beneficiary of globalization. It has been correspondingly badly hit by the decline in exports, which has also spread to the domestic consumer market. Its financial system, however, has remained largely unaffected by the global turmoil, and it is sitting on the largest currency reserves in the world. This gives China a broader range of policy options than most other countries have.

What China decides to do will have almost as much influence on the future of the global economy as President Obama, and the China–United States bilateral relationship will be the most important in the world. China has a tremendous interest in the prosperity of the global economy. This is something on which President Obama can build in reconstructing the international financial system, but it will require great tact and foresight on both sides.

The emergence of a new world power is a very dangerous process. Twice it has led to world war in which the emergent power was defeated. The transition from the United Kingdom to the United States was the exception. It was peacefully accomplished, but the two countries speak the same language. The United States and China have vastly different languages and cultures. China has long been regarded with fear and suspicion in the West. China has to go out of its way to make itself acceptable if it wants to be welcomed as a world leader. It has adopted the doctrine of harmonious development, which is the right approach, but it also has other doctrines, notably those relating to Taiwan and Tibet, that work in the opposite direction. Due to the erroneous policies of the Bush administration and the bursting of the super-bubble, China has gained too much power too soon. For a constructive partnership, both sides will have to bend over backward. President Obama has to treat China as an equal partner, and China has to accept continuing American leadership. This will not be easy for either side.

China has much to lose. It is not a democracy, and there is no established routine for changing governments. Failure to achieve a satisfactory growth rate—generally defined as 8 percent per annum—could easily lead to political turmoil, and political turmoil in China would be disastrous for the world. Fortunately, China has developed a method of elaborate consultations that, while not democratic, do give the various interest groups involved a voice in determining policy. The main drawback of the consensus-building process is that it is slow and cumbersome; there is a danger that the Chinese leadership will not move fast enough to counteract the sudden drop in the global economy. Here again, a strong lead from the new Obama administration could have a beneficial effect. I expect China to go through a steep but short recession, reaching the bottom around the middle of 2009 and rebounding strongly enough to approach 8 percent growth for 2009 as a whole.

THE INDIAN SUBCONTINENT

India is more self-contained than China, and it should have less difficulty in maintaining its upside momentum. The removal of inflationary pressures should go part of the way toward offsetting the decline in exports. The Indian stock market has been harder hit than that of most countries, but its financial system, which is still largely under government influence, has been less affected. Remittances from the Gulf States will suffer, and its outsourcing business will languish, but hopefully infrastructure investments, of which India has a great backlog, will continue apace. The macro-economic outlook is more favorable for India than for most of the world. The greatest uncertainties are political, and they revolve around Pakistan.

Pakistan is a failing state. Some elements in the military and intelligence services have been closely involved with terrorists, and there is a real danger that they may gain the upper hand. The November 26, 2008, terrorist attacks on Mumbai were brilliantly planned, timed, and executed. It may not be the work of the same people who planned September 11, but it is the product of the same kind of thinking. Coming before the Indian elections, it was meant to set India and Pakistan against each other, allowing the Islamist influence in Pakistan at least to survive or at most to gain control of the State. The situation is extremely complicated and poses the greatest diplomatic and security challenge to the Obama administration. The Bush administration has allowed all the various players to be set against each other—Pakistan against India and Afghanistan; the military against the civilian government within Pakistan; Nawaz Sharif against Asif Ali Zardari, within the civilian government—and the various tribes that have been armed by the military in order to fight the Pakistani Taliban may start fighting each other. The task of the Obama administration will be to bring the various factions together to fight their common enemy, the Islamist terrorists in Pakistan.

The problem of Pakistan is closely interlinked with the problem of Afghanistan. The American forces invading Afghanistan were originally welcomed as liberators; the political transition was also well prepared with the loya jirga (constitutional assembly). But NATO got involved without a proper plan of engagement, and after eight years the presence of foreign troops is no longer welcome. A new NATO plan ought to call for an orderly exit, but that is not possible while al Qaeda and the Taliban are gathering strength. Yet they cannot be defeated without the active support of the local population. That is the quandary that confronts the incoming administration. Specifically, three obstacles stand in the way of success: the drug war that sets the local population against the occupying powers, the existence of a safe haven in the tribal areas of Pakistan, and the loss of legitimacy and popularity of the Hamid Karzai regime. The situation is not insoluble, but it will require extraordinary skill and perseverance to bring it under control.

THE OIL-PRODUCING COUNTRIES

The oil-producing countries have suffered a sudden reversal of fortune. Their surpluses have turned into deficits, and their sovereign wealth funds and currency reserves have suffered major losses. The Gulf States have been badly hit because their private sectors, including some banks, were greatly overextended. Dubai was the world's most spectacular real estate bubble, and it will have to be rescued by the deep pockets of Abu Dhabi.

But the oil producers' woes are not necessarily bad news. Some of the major oil-surplus countries, notably Iran, Venezuela, and Russia, have been enemies of the current world order, and their wings are being clipped—it is difficult to sponsor Bolivarian revolutions with oil at $40 a barrel. The decline in Iran's capacity to sponsor political and terrorist movements in neighboring countries is already having beneficial effects. The political and security situations in Iraq seem to be stabilizing, and Syria seems to be more amenable to negotiation. The chances are good that Iranian President Mahmoud Ahmadinejad will not be re-elected in June 2009 and that a somewhat more reasonable leadership will come to the fore, allowing for negotiations.

The ground was subtly shifting in the Middle East, providing some hope for an eventual settlement of the

Israeli-Palestinian conflict before the militant approach that characterized the Bush Era had its last fling with the Israeli incursion into Gaza that began on December 27, 2008. What seemed to be an improving situation suddenly turned critical. While Israel was inflicting military damage on Hamas, the killing of civilians was influencing public opinion and raising the specter of civil unrest in Egypt and other Muslim countries. Early moves by Barack Obama, including his appointment of George Mitchell as special envoy and his interview on Al Arabiya, have sent an unmistakable message that he intends to take a different approach.

In contrast to Venezuela and Iran, Russia may become more of a menace as a result of the decline in oil prices. Under Vladimir Putin, nationalism has replaced communism as the country's guiding ideology. Those in the Kremlin are now using control over natural resources to reestablish Russia's position as a political power, to enrich themselves, and to gain control of the natural resources of former Soviet republics by enriching their rulers personally. The various objectives mutually reinforce each other; together, they constitute the new order—a sham democracy built on petrol patronage.

In the Putin regime, economic power has been concentrated in the hands of two groups: those who acquired property and those who take a slice of cash flows. By and large, the first group is more sophisticated and more Western oriented; it keeps its money and its children abroad. The second group exploits the state's arbitrary powers more directly. The first group was decimated by the financial crisis; the second was left relatively unscathed. The net effect has been to reinforce the tendency of the state to use arbitrary power rather than to rely on the rule of law. For example, a large portion of official currency reserves was spent to bail out and reacquire the first group's assets.

As the economic outlook deteriorates, the Putin regime will be unable to satisfy people's economic expectations, and it is likely to rely more actively on arbitrary state powers. After all, the Kremlin is occupied not by the cautious bureaucrats of the Soviet era but by buccaneers who were willing to take risks to get where they are. This may translate into military adventures abroad and repression at home. Already, two prominent political opponents were recently assassinated, and a proposed law treats any association with a foreign NGO as treason.

EUROPE'S RUSSIA PROBLEM

I have strong views on Russia because of my deep personal involvement. When Mikhail Gorbachev telephoned Andrey Sakharov in his exile in Gorki at the end of 1986 and asked him to return to Moscow "to resume his patriotic activities" I felt that the Soviet Union was ready for change. I visited the country in the spring of 1987 and set up a foundation there that became quite influential in promoting democracy and open society. My efforts were greatly appreciated and warmly supported, particularly by the foreign ministry of the Soviet Union, which was at that time the sector of the Soviet bureaucracy most in favor of perestroika. Although I was quite unknown at the time, I was encouraged to set up an international task force to prepare for the establishment of an "open sector" in the economy. The project came to naught because the centrally planned economy was already too diseased to sustain the embryo of a market-oriented economy.

In the spring of 1989, I addressed an East-West conference in Potsdam, which was then still part of East Germany, pleading for a Marshall Plan for the Soviet Union that would be financed mainly by the European countries. My proposal was greeted with loud laughter led by a junior minister in Margaret Thatcher's government. Subsequently, I shepherded a delegation of young economists led by Grigory Yavlinsky through the annual meeting of the World Bank and the IMF in Washington in October 1990. They advocated a five-hundred-day program (originally called the Shatalin Plan) for dissolving the Soviet Union and replacing it with an economic union modeled on the European Common Market. They failed to drum up any international endorsement of that plan, and after their return Gorbachev decided against pursuing it.*

Eventually the Soviet Union broke up in a disorderly manner. The Western powers in turn decided to delegate the task of assisting the Soviet Union and its successor states to the IMF, because they did not want to put any burden on their own budgets. The IMF was ill-suited to the task. It operated by getting the governments of the countries seeking its assistance to sign a letter of intent and then relying on those governments to execute the programs. But neither the Soviet Union nor Russia (nor any of the other successor states) had functioning governments capable of executing an IMF program at the time. One program after another failed,

---

*For a more detailed account, see my *Opening the Soviet System* (London: Weidenfeld & Nicolson), 1990, or *Underwriting Democracy: Encouraging Free Enterprise and Democratic Reform among the Soviets in Eastern Europe* (New York: PublicAffairs, 2004).

and Russia passed through a period of political, economic, social, and moral breakdown.

My foundation, which by that time covered the entire former Soviet empire, did what it could in the fields of culture, education, media, civil society, and the rule of law, although its impact was insignificant in relation to the magnitude of the problems. The field of science, where it threw a lifeline to more than thirty thousand leading scientists, constituted an exception. Had the West engaged in an aid program along similar lines but on a larger scale, it would have been greatly appreciated in Russia at that time, and history would have taken a different course.

When Vladimir Putin succeeded Boris Yeltsin as president, he managed to forge a new order out of the chaos, but it turned out to have too many similarities with the old order. Hopes of establishing a Western-style democracy went unfulfilled. The Western powers had failed to live up to the exaggerated expectations that Russian reformers attached to them. The West made hardly any efforts or sacrifices to implant Western values in Russia; it merely used the weakness of Russia to extend its sphere of influence farther to the East. This is a historical fact that has left an indelible mark on Russian attitudes but is not recognized in the West. Nothing that the West does now can alter history. Rightly or wrongly, both the Russian rulers and the Russian public harbor a deeply felt resentment towards the West for the way they were treated in their times of trouble. The resentment is most strongly felt by those who were yearning for a Western-style democracy.

The Kremlin's geopolitical power game led to armed conflict with Georgia in August 2008. Its roots go back to

Georgia's Revolution of the Roses in 2003, which was followed by Ukraine's Orange Revolution. Successful revolts against corrupt and inept regimes posed a potent challenge to the new order and made the Kremlin very nervous. And Georgia stood in the way of the Kremlin's geopolitical ambition to reassert control over the former Soviet republics and thereby extend its control over Europe's oil and gas supplies. In addition, Putin and Georgia's president, Mikheil Saakashvili, developed great personal animosity towards each other.

Anticipating Russian aggression, Saakashvili built up Georgia's defense forces. The use of slush funds bred corruption, and corruption led to other excesses. The Saakashvili regime lost its luster as a shining example of democracy and open society. But in the winter of 2006–2007, when Russia preemptively cut off gas supplies to both Georgia and Ukraine—and in the case of Georgia also blew up the electricity line—Georgia fended off the attack more successfully than Ukraine. Saakashvili became the darling of the Bush administration. He was hailed as a champion of democracy, but he was never held to account for his transgressions against the rule of law. On the contrary, the Bush administration actively promoted Georgia's membership application to NATO.

Success went to Saakashvili's head. Against all advice, he responded to Russian provocation in South Ossetia by mounting a military attack in August 2008. Russia applied overwhelming force and crushed Georgia militarily. Exactly how the events unfolded is still shrouded in mystery, and it would be helpful if a fact-finding commission could clarify them. As it stands, the Russians had some excuse for taking military action, although the Russian citizens they claimed to be protecting were really South Ossetians who had been only recently given Russian citizenship. The Russians launched a propaganda campaign concurrently with the military one and managed to divide European public opinion.

The armistice negotiated by Nicolas Sarkozy, as E.U. president, recognized Russia's military dominance. It allowed Russian "peacekeepers" to roam deeply into Georgian territory, where they wreaked havoc with Georgia's military capacity. The military position Russia now occupies in an expanded South Ossetia directly threatens the Baku-Ceyhan pipeline and greatly reduces Georgia's reliability as a connecting link to the oil and gas resources of Central Asia. This tilted the geopolitical balance in favor of Russia. Russia now has more power and influence over Europe than it ever did during the Cold War.

Reasserting Russia's geopolitical importance also made Putin very popular with the Russian public, and so did baiting the West. The invasion of Georgia was both a political and a military success—but it had unintended adverse financial consequences. Capital fled Russia. The stock market fell precipitously and the ruble weakened. Coming at a time of global financial turmoil, the consequences were disastrous. Margin calls proliferated and exposed a fatal flaw in the Putin regime: Businessmen had no confidence in the regime because of its arbitrary character. They kept their money abroad and operated their businesses with borrowed money. The margin calls resulted in a spate of defaults that changed the economic landscape. Industrial production is falling, and—consumption being based largely on imports—living standards are being adversely affected by the weakness of the ruble. As the economy deteriorates, the Putin regime is liable to turn increasingly agressive to Europe and repressive at home.

How should Europe react to the rise of a hostile Russia on its eastern flank? Different countries have reacted differently, influenced by their historical experience and their economic interests. Yet it is essential for the European Union to develop a unified policy towards Russia, reconciling these divergent national interests and attitudes. Europe cannot afford not to resist Russia's geopolitical aggression, and it needs to be unified to have any chance of success. Yet, the unified European policy must not be purely geopolitical, because if it were, the common interest would not be strong enough to override national interests. Russia could divide and conquer, as it is doing already. In purely geopolitical terms, Russia holds the stronger hand. Europe's superiority lies in its values and principles as an open, democratic, peaceful, prosperous, and law-abiding society. These values hold great attraction for the people in the former Soviet Union— and that includes the leaders as well as the masses, in spite of the fact that the West did not back up its values and principles with deeds in the past. As a result, admiration of and aspiration to European values is mixed with disillusionment and resentment.

Nevertheless, Russia remains susceptible to Europe's allure. Historically, Russia has always aspired to be part of Europe, and the Putin regime recognizes that it cannot afford to revert to the Soviet Union's isolation. Russia's strengthened geopolitical position vis-à-vis Europe obscures grave weaknesses in other areas. Its authoritarian political system stifles private enterprise and innovation. The rule of law is absent, and much more effort is spent on extortion and rent collection than production. Consequently, economic progress has not kept pace with the accumulation of oil revenues. These deficiencies became accentuated by the decline in the price of oil.

Another great weakness is demographic: Russia has immense territory but only 140 million people. A growing portion of the population consists of Muslim minorities with higher birthrates than ethnic Russians. Overall population is expected to drop by 10 million in a decade. Resource-rich but sparsely populated Siberia is bordered by resource-deficient but teeming and rising China. If the Central Asian republics are cut off from the West, they are liable to turn to China in order to avoid becoming totally dependent on Russia. In the long run, Putin's baiting of the West may turn out to be as self-defeating as Saakashvili's baiting of Russia. But in the short run there is a real danger that Russia will pursue its age-old desire to be part of Europe by seeking to become the dominant entity.

In these circumstances, Europe needs to pursue a two-pronged strategy. On the one hand, it must protect itself against the geopolitical threat posed by a newly assertive and adventurous Russia. On the other, it must seek to replace the rule of force with the rule of law, and geopolitics with the pursuit of democracy, open society, and international cooperation. The European Union could not possibly forge a common policy without such a two-pronged approach. There would be too many freeloaders and defectors in a purely geopolitical game, but in a two-pronged approach each member state could find its proper place.

The key to neutralizing the geopolitical advantage that Russia enjoys is to establish a unified energy policy with a

Europewide regulatory authority that has precedence over national regulators, and a Europewide distribution network. This would deprive Russia of its ability to play one country against another, because a concession granted to one national distributor would immediately become available to customers in all the other countries. Energy companies are beginning to realize this and becoming less resistant to a European energy policy. That would also serve another shared objective, namely helping to bring climate change under control.

The other prong—promoting the rule of law, international cooperation, and the principles of open society—has to be pursued indirectly, by reforming the international financial system and by paying special attention to Russia's near-abroad. Ukraine, in particular, is in a perilous state, but financing public works that would create jobs in Eastern Ukraine, where the steel industry is in distress, could make a major difference both politically and economically. Georgia must also be helped to recover from the damage inflicted by the Russian invasion, but help should be contingent on the Saakashvili regime observing the principles of open society. Russia cannot be helped directly because of its excessive reliance on arbitrary state power, but when Russia sees progress in international cooperation, particularly with China, it will not want to be left out in the cold.

Strengthening and supporting the former Soviet republics would serve both prongs of a unified policy towards Russia. It would be against open society values if Russia were allowed to turn them into satellites just because it has superior military force. And Europe has a geopolitical interest in keeping them open as sources of energy supply.

Europe's Internal Problems

The financial crisis and its aftermath will be a period of testing, and hopefully development, for the institutions of the European Union. That is particularly true of its financial institutions. These are relatively new and not fully developed. Europe has a common currency and the European Central Bank, but it does not have a common fiscal policy or treasury. This shortcoming became evident in the aftermath of the Lehman Brothers bankruptcy, when confidence in the entire banking system was shaken. The leadership of Europe, most prominently Gordon Brown, recognized the emergency but lacked the institutional framework for dealing with it. On the Sunday of the annual meeting of the IMF, October 12, 2008, the European finance ministers held an emergency meeting in Paris and resolved to effectively guarantee the integrity of their financial systems. After a heated debate in which Germany resisted a Europewide solution, it was decided that each country should guarantee its own financial system. This was an incomplete step forward, but it worked for a while because it was generally believed that if it proved inadequate—for instance, if Ireland or Switzerland got into difficulties—additional steps would be taken. As an unintended and unanticipated side effect, the currencies and bond markets of the new member countries that have not yet joined the euro—Hungary in particular—came under severe pressure and had to be rescued with an IMF program and swap lines from the ECB and the Bank of England.

These events demonstrated the benefits of belonging to the euro. Greece is hurting less than Denmark, although its problems are much worse. A majority of the European public now believes that the euro will become more important as an international reserve currency than the dollar. But since the beginning of 2009, the shortcomings of European financial arrangements have become more evident by the minute. As noted previously, Germany and the ECB have adopted a radically different posture from the rest of the world, and this is causing policy conflicts within Europe. Differences in economic and financial conditions within the eurozone between the southern-tier countries and Ireland, on the one hand, and Germany, on the other, are disturbing. Several of the former have been downgraded by the rating agencies, and the spreads among government bonds have widened to an alarming extent.

The fact that the regulation of banks is in the hands of national authorities, not a Europewide one, is liable to lead to beggar-thy-neighbor policies. For example, Austrian or Italian regulators may induce their banks to cut back on lending to Eastern Europe, causing problems for those countries. Regulation ought to transcend narrow national interests, but only an incipient crisis will generate the necessary political will. That crisis is now brewing. The outcome is uncertain, but given the proven benefits of a common currency, it is to be expected that the euro will emerge with its institutions strengthened. The ECB is likely to end up with increased regulatory powers over the banking system and greater backing from the Treasuries of the member countries.

The Bush administration distinguished itself by driving a wedge between "old Europe" and "new Europe." It is to be hoped that the Obama administration will adopt a more constructive course. The world badly needs a more united Europe both politically and financially.

THE REST OF THE DEVELOPING WORLD

A few countries, such as Brazil and Chile, are reasonably well positioned to engage in countercyclical policies largely on their own with only a light assist from the IFIs. But most of the rest of the developing world is heavily dependent on the initiatives outlined in the previous chapter. In the absence of a radical international initiative, they face a very grim future. Countries such as Pakistan, Egypt, Morocco, and Haiti have already experienced food riots. Others, such as South Africa and Turkey, suffer from serious power outages. Mexico has a serious security problem because of drug trafficking. As the economic situation deteriorates, the chances of civil unrest rise.

The collapse of credit in the global financial system is having an even more devastating effect on the countries at the periphery than those at the center. Credit lines have been withdrawn, maturing loans cannot be rolled over, and trade finance has dried up. Hopefully, the leaders of the developed world recognize that it is in their own enlightened self-interest to come to the rescue of the developing world. The attraction of the SDR donation scheme is that it does not impose any direct costs on donor countries. All they have to do is vote for the creation of SDR and then pass on the benefits to less-developed countries. I hope they will rise to the occasion.

CHAPTER 12

The Fate of the New Paradigm

Since my book was first published, we have lived through a remarkable historical episode. A very powerful pervasive structure that we take for granted, the global financial system, has actually collapsed. This is a shocking experience particularly for those who haven't lived through anything like it before. That is true of most people in the United States. I was somewhat better prepared because I had the dubious privilege of living through the Nazi occupation of Budapest as a Jew in my youth. This led me to develop a conceptual framework which is useful for understanding exactly this kind of episode. The framework deals with a much broader subject than the financial market, namely the two-way, reflexive relationship between the participants' thinking and the situation in which they participate—but the financial markets provide an excellent laboratory for studying the subject and testing my theories. Indeed, I originally wrote this book because I thought the unfolding financial crisis would offer an excellent opportunity to demonstrate the validity and relevance of my conceptual framework, the main contention of which is that misconceptions play an important role in shaping history. It would be hard to find a more convincing demonstration than the Crash of 2008.

The book provides some valuable insights—notably the super-bubble hypothesis—to explain what was happening and to foreshadow what was in store. Yet the theory of reflexivity did not receive the kind of acceptance that I believe it deserves. The word "reflexivity" came to be widely used, but the implications of the concept were not explored and its meaning was not properly understood. Indeed, one cannot call reflexivity "the new paradigm" because to qualify as a paradigm it would have to be widely used as the basis for research agenda. That has not happened.

The prevailing interpretation of financial markets—the Efficient Market Hypothesis (EMH)—has been well and truly discredited by the Crash of 2008. The current financial crisis was not caused by some exogenous factor—like the formation or dissolution of an oil cartel—but by the financial system itself. This puts the lie to the assertion that financial markets tend towards equilibrium and deviations are caused by external shocks. But the alternative theory of how markets work that I am proposing—the theory of reflexivity—has not taken its place. It has not even received serious consideration by the economics profession.

When I ask why, I get various answers. One is that my theory of reflexivity merely states the obvious, namely that market prices reflect the participants' biases. That is an obvious misunderstanding of my theory, which holds that mispricing in financial markets can, in specific circumstances and ways, affect the fundamentals that market prices are supposed to reflect. Other experts say that my theory of bubbles is already incorporated in existing models.

Those who are most sympathetic to my views explain to me that my theory is not getting more attention because it cannot be formalized and modeled. But that is exactly the point I am trying to make: Reflexivity gives rise to uncertainties that cannot be quantified and probabilities that cannot be calculated. Frank Knight made that point a century ago in *Risk, Uncertainty and Profit*, and John Maynard Keynes recognized it too. Yet market participants, rating agencies, and regulators alike came to depend on quantitative models in calculating risks.

One question I am seeking an answer to is whether it is possible to model reflexivity, or whether one should continue using quantitative models but take reflexivity into account by adding a margin for error due to incalculable uncertainties. My hunch is that we need to do both. Reflexivity cannot be modeled in the abstract, but it should be possible to model specific instances of it, such as the effect of the willingness to lend on real estate prices. At the same time, quantitative models may be useful for calculating the risks that prevail in near-equilibrium conditions while remembering, particularly for regulatory purposes, that conditions may occasionally veer quite far away from equilibrium. These are questions which need to be explored.

Insofar as there is a new paradigm emerging to explain how markets work, it is based on behavioral economics and evolutionary systems theory. I have followed their development with great interest, and I recognize their merits; yet I worry that they leave out some important insights. I believe that it would stand in the way of a proper understanding of financial markets if they became the new orthodoxy. Let me explain why.

Behavioral economics explores the quirks of human behavior and its implications for market behavior. It has demonstrated through experiments a number of departures from rational behavior in the form of specific behavioral biases that are characteristic of decision making under conditions of uncertainty, and that are detrimental to the agent's own best economic interests. This has challenged the assumption of rational behavior and the EMH. The supporters of the EMH have responded by admitting the existence of these inefficiencies, but they claim that they can be eliminated by arbitrage.

This assertion has provided the justification for so-called market-neutral hedge funds, which claim to be able to make high profits by exploiting arbitrage opportunities on a leveraged basis. The most famous example is Long Term Capital Management (LTCM), which blew up in 1998, nearly causing a meltdown in financial markets. Behavioral economics has no explanation for why LTCM blew up. More precisely, its implied explanation is that the forces of behavioral bias proved stronger than LTCM's capacity to withstand them. That is far less satisfactory than the concept of self-reinforcing biases, or bubbles, that I put forward.

Indeed, the charge leveled against reflexivity—that it merely states the obvious fact that human psychology affects market prices—can more justifiably be raised against behavioral economics. What would be lost if it became the new paradigm is the insight that mispricing can affect the fundamentals, and that financial markets, far from being merely passive reflections of underlying conditions, constitute an active force that changes the course of history.

Markets often force managements, and even governments, to act in specific ways to address their concerns. Even in exploring human psychology, behavioral economics is more rudimentary than my theory: It explores only behavioral biases, not misconceptions like market fundamentalism. It is also more rudimentary than the EMH, because it does not formulate any overarching hypothesis.

By contrast, evolutionary systems theory does formulate an overarching hypothesis. Andrew W. Lo of MIT has formalized this approach as the Adaptive Markets Hypothesis (AMH), and he is not alone. The Santa Fe Institute is heading in the same direction. Indeed, it has become very fashionable to apply Charles Darwin's concept of the survival of the fittest to as many domains as possible.

The AMH views financial markets as an ecosystem in which participants pursuing different strategies compete with each other to maximize the survival rate of their genetic material, that is, profits. It escapes the constraints of the EMH by admitting any strategy as long as it promotes survival.

The AMH has the great merit that it can be modeled, and the models are dynamic: Both the strategies and their prevalence evolve in the course of iteration. The concept of equilibrium can be replaced by a two-way interaction akin to reflexivity. This modeling technique has been developed in studying the two-way relationship between populations of predators and prey, and there it works very well. Since then, such "adaptive" models have spread to many subjects in addition to financial markets, including the study of religion.

Obviously, the AMH has great affinity with reflexivity. I am fascinated by it, and I hope that it may provide a way to model reflexivity—which seems to be the main obstacle to my conceptual framework being taken seriously. Yet I also dread it. I am afraid that my insights may be distorted in the process of being adapted to a modeling technique. Let me try to articulate my fears.

Central to my worldview is the idea that human affairs—events with thinking participants—have a fundamentally different structure from natural phenomena. The latter unfold without any interference from human thought; one set of facts follows another in the causal chain. Not so in human affairs. The causal chain does not lead from one set of facts to the next, but connects the situation and the participants' thinking in a two-way, reflexive feedback loop.

Since there is always a divergence between the participants' views and the actual state of affairs, reflexivity introduces an element of uncertainty into the course of events that is absent in natural phenomena. I am afraid this idea may get lost in the AMH, because evolutionary systems theory does not distinguish between human and natural phenomena. It deals with the evolution of populations whether they consist of microbes or market participants.

To be even more specific: I draw a distinction between machines such as automobiles and power plants, on the one hand, and social institutions such as states or markets or matrimonial arrangements, on the other. I contend that machines need to be well formed in order to survive, that is, they must do the job for which they were designed. Social institutions are different: They may not serve their purpose well, yet they may survive indefinitely. In other words, markets may be maladaptive. This is the distinction that the AMH fails to recognize.

There is something suspicious about the concept of adaptive systems, whether we talk about markets or governments or religions. It seems to justify whatever prevails merely because it prevails. That ignores the most important lesson to be learned from the Crash of 2008. An immensely impressive and imposing edifice, the international financial system, collapsed not because of some extraneous shock, but because it was ill conceived. How was that possible?

There has to be some difference between social constructs like the banking system and physical constructs like the buildings resembling Greek temples in which banks used to be located. Market participants, including regulators, discovered this truth at great cost and with great consternation in the Crash of 2008; the world economy is reeling from the consequences. My conceptual framework identifies what the difference between mechanical and social constructs is, namely reflexivity. The AMH fails to acknowledge that there is any difference at all, and thus perpetuates the root error of the EMH.

How could economics produce two hypotheses that suffer from the same error? The explanation lies in the fact that both the EMH and the AMH proceed by analogy, applying to the social sphere an approach that was successful in another field—the EMH draws on Newtonian physics, the AMH on evolutionary biology. In this context, I should like to invoke my postulate of radical fallibility: Whenever we acquire some useful knowledge, we tend to extend it to areas where it is no longer applicable.

By contrast, I start with an exploration of the relationship between thinking and reality. That is how I arrive at the concept of reflexivity, which can then be applied to the study of financial markets. I contend that my approach produces better results than either the EMH or the AMH, and I expressly repudiate any attempt to reconcile my conclusions with either of those hypotheses. Since the EMH has been thoroughly discredited, I am more worried about being overshadowed by the AMH, which is ascendant.

I understand the motivation behind the AMH: the desire to protect the scientific status of economics. But I consider that a misplaced endeavor, the product of what in Freudian terms might be described as economists' "physics envy." I contend that the social and natural sciences face different tasks and require different approaches.

Here, I must introduce a cautionary note about my own argument. I am troubled by the sharp distinction that I have drawn between human affairs and natural phenomena. Such sharp dividing lines are not characteristic of nature, but of human efforts to make sense of an infinitely complicated reality. This is also in accordance with my postulate of radical fallibility.

Nevertheless, I am eager to understand better the connection between evolutionary systems theory and reflexivity. I posed the question at the Santa Fe Institute, which is devoted to the study of complexity, but I have not yet found the answer. That is another question I wish other people would think about.

I am willing to admit that reflexivity does not meet the currently accepted standards of scientific theory. That is why I called my first book on the subject *The Alchemy of Finance*. I contend, however, that we must either modify the standards or study financial markets in a nonscientific way, which may be difficult, because it would involve a loss of status for economists.

It may be easier to gain acceptance for the new paradigm by calling it a philosophical rather than a scientific paradigm. Philosophy used to occupy a preeminent position before scientific method took its place. Scientific method has worked wonders in the study of nature, but it has been less successful in the human domain. That is what led me to take issue with Karl Popper's doctrine of the unity of scientific method.

It may be appropriate to restore philosophy to its preeminent position. My conceptual framework could then serve as the new philosophical paradigm for understanding human affairs in general and financial markets in particular. I happen to be more interested in its philosophical implications than its financial implications, although it would be disingenuous of me to downplay the latter. There is a lot more to be said on both topics. I must stop here, but I do not consider this the end of the discussion.

Conclusion

My main purpose in writing this book is to demonstrate the validity and importance of reflexivity. The moment is auspicious. Not only has the prevailing paradigm—equilibrium theory, and its political derivative, market fundamentalism—proven itself incapable of explaining the current state of affairs, it can be held responsible for landing us in the mess we are in. We badly need a new paradigm. But the new paradigm I am proposing—the recognition of reflexivity—still has to prove its worth. Until now it could not compete with equilibrium theory because it could not provide unequivocal predictions. That is why it was not given any serious consideration by economists. Now that equilibrium theory has shown itself to be such a failure at both prediction and explanation, the field is more open. The idea that reflexivity introduces an element of uncertainty into human affairs in general and financial markets in particular must be given some credence. But the theory must still show what it can do. I have done what I can by way of explanation. I have also used my conceptual framework to guide me in my investment decisions. Still, I believe I could do more in drawing on that framework as well as a lifetime of experience (the two are interconnected) to figure out what lies ahead. I claim that we are at the end of an era. What will the new era look like?

Firm predictions are out of the question. The future depends on the policy responses the financial crisis will provoke. But we can identify the problems and analyze the policy options. We can also make some firm predictions about what the next era will *not* look like. The post–World War II period of credit expansion will not be followed by an equally long period of credit contraction. Boom-bust processes are asymmetric in shape: a long, gradually accelerating boom is followed by a short and sharp bust. Consequently, most of the credit contraction can be expected to occur in the near term. House prices have already declined nearly 10 percent, and they are liable to decline another 20 percent or more in the next year. The deleveraging of hedge funds and bank balance sheets is also in full swing; it cannot continue at the current rate much longer. It may receive new impetus from a recession or other dislocations; nevertheless, it can be expected to run its course within a year or so. The end of the credit contraction is liable to bring some short-term relief, but it is unlikely to be followed by a resumption of credit expansion at anything like the rates to which we have become accustomed.

While a recession in the United States is now (April 2008) inevitable, there is no reason yet to expect a global recession. Powerful expansionary forces are at work in other parts of the world, and they may well counterbalance a recession in the United States and a slowdown in Europe and Japan. Economic developments may of course have political repercussions that could disrupt the world economy.

In the same vein, the end of the super-bubble does not mean the end of all bubbles. On the contrary, new bubbles are already in formation. The flight from the dollar has reinforced an already extended boom in raw materials and energy. Biofuel legislation has generated a boom in agricultural products. And the appreciation of the renminbi has caused real interest rates in China to turn negative, and that is usually associated with an asset bubble.

So what does the end of an era really mean? I contend that it means the end of a long period of relative stability based on the United States as the dominant power and the dollar as the main international reserve currency. I foresee a period of political and financial instability, hopefully to be followed by the emergence of a new world order.

To appreciate what is in store I have to explain one of the corollaries of my conceptual framework to which I have not given sufficient emphasis until now. I have spoken of the postulate of radical fallibility, the idea that all human constructs are flawed in one way or another, although the flaws may not become apparent until a construct has been in existence for a while. It follows that flawed constructs can be stable for extended periods. I have also spoken of a fundamental difference between natural and social science. One of the ways in which the difference manifests itself is that machines that utilize the forces of nature must obey the laws of nature; they must be what analytical philosophers call "well formed." Power stations must produce electricity, combustion engines must burn fuel in a controlled manner, nuclear weapons must release the energy contained in the nuclei of atoms in an explosion, and so on. Social arrangements need not deliver on their promises in the same way; it is enough if people can be persuaded to accept them for one reason or another, be it persuasion, tradition, or compulsion. Indeed, social arrangements can never be "well formed" because of the innate inability of participants to base their decisions purely on knowledge. Whatever regime prevails, it is liable to contain unresolved contradictions, and it may be succeeded by a totally different regime in short order.

What I am trying to explain in this abstract manner I have experienced in a very tangible form during my lifetime. I grew up in a stable, middle-class environment; then the Nazis would have killed me if my father had not arranged for me a false identity. I experienced the beginnings of Communist repression in Hungary; then I was an outsider in England, looking in on a stable, self-contained society. I saw the financial markets transformed out of all recognition in the course of fifty years, and I became somebody out of a nobody.

As I look at history, I see stable periods come and go. Now I see a relatively stable period going. I can identify enormous inconsistencies in the prevailing arrangements. They are not new; indeed they are inevitable in the sense that no arrangements are known that would avoid them. Take the exchange rate system. Every currency regime has its shortcomings. Fixed exchange rates are too rigid and prone to break down; floating exchange rates tend to swing too much; managed floats and crawling pegs tend to reinforce the trend they seek to moderate. I used to joke that currency regimes resemble matrimonial regimes: Whatever regime prevails, its opposite looks more attractive. Or consider the prevailing world order. There is something inconsistent about a globalized economy and political arrangements based on the principle of sovereignty. These inconsistencies were present in the era which is now coming to an end, but the dominance of the United States and the dollar introduced a sense of stability. Something has happened to disrupt that stability. The policies pursued by the Bush administration have impaired the political dominance of the United States, and now a financial crisis has endangered the international financial system and reduced the willingness of the rest of the world to hold dollars.

In my boom-bust model, far-from-equilibrium conditions are characteristic of the later stages of a bubble, to be followed by a return to more normal, near-equilibrium conditions. In this respect the super-bubble does not follow my boom-bust model, because there are no normal, near-equilibrium conditions to return to. We are facing a period of greatly increased uncertainty where the range of possible outcomes is much broader than in normal times. The greatest uncertainty revolves around the response of the U.S. authorities to the predicament that confronts them.

The United States is facing both a recession and a flight from the dollar. The decline in housing prices, the weight of accumulated household debt, and the losses and uncertainties in the banking system threaten to push the economy into a self-reinforcing decline. Measures to combat this threat increase the supply of dollars. At the same time, the flight from the dollar has set up inflationary pressures through higher energy, commodity, and food prices. The European Central Bank, whose mission is to maintain price stability, is reluctant to lower interest rates. This has created a discord between U.S. and E.U. monetary policy and put upward pressure on the euro. The euro has appreciated more than the renminbi, creating trade tension between Europe and China. The renminbi can be expected to catch up with the euro both to avoid protectionism in the United States and increasingly in Europe, and to contain imported price inflation in China. This will, in turn, increase prices at Wal-Mart and put additional pressure on the already beleaguered U.S. consumer. Unfortunately this administration shows no understanding of the predicament in which it finds itself.

Eventually, the U.S. government will have to use taxpayers' money to arrest the decline in house prices. Until it does, the decline will be self-reinforcing, with people walking away from homes in which they have negative equity and more and more financial institutions becoming insolvent, thus reinforcing both the recession and flight from the dollar. The Bush administration and most economic forecasters do not understand that markets can be self-reinforcing on the downside as well as the upside. They are waiting for the housing market to find a bottom on its own, but it is further away than they think. The Bush administration resists using taxpayers' money because of its market fundamentalist ideology and its reluctance to yield power to Congress. It has left the conduct of policy largely to the Federal Reserve. This has put too much of a burden on an institution designed to deal with liquidity, not solvency, problems. With the Bear Stearns rescue operation and the latest-term security lending facility, the Fed has put its own balance sheet at risk. I expect better of the next administration. Until then, I foresee many policy turns and changes in market direction since current policies are inadequate. It will be difficult to stay ahead of the curve.

*   *   *

I release this book at the present time with grave misgivings. I am afraid that there will be a conflict between my interest in writing the book and the interest of those who will read it, particularly in the electronic edition. Near panic conditions prevail in financial markets. People want to know what lies ahead. I cannot tell them because I do not know.

What I want to tell them is something different. I want to explain the human condition.

We have to make decisions without having sufficient knowledge at our disposal. We have gained control over the forces of nature. That makes us very powerful. Our decisions have great impact. We can do a lot of good or a lot of harm. But we have not learned how to govern ourselves. As a consequence, we live in great uncertainty and grave danger. We need to gain a better understanding of the situation in which we find ourselves. It is difficult to accept uncertainty. It is tempting to try and escape it by kidding ourselves and each other, but that is liable to land us in greater difficulties.

My life has been devoted to gaining a better understanding of reality. In this book I have focused on the financial markets because they provide an excellent laboratory for testing my theories, and I have rushed into print because this is a moment when a prevailing misconception has landed us in grave difficulties. This should at least demonstrate how important it is to confront reality instead of trying to escape it. We can, of course, never fully comprehend reality, and I do not pretend that reflexivity constitutes the ultimate truth. The theory claims that the ultimate truth is beyond our human reach and explores the role that misconceptions play in shaping the course of events. That is not what people are interested in when financial markets are in turmoil. But I hope they will be willing to give it some consideration. In return, I hope I have given them some insight into what goes on in the financial markets.

I should like to end with a plea. Let this not be the conclusion but the beginning of a concerted effort at better understanding the human condition. Given our increased

control over the forces of nature, how can we govern ourselves better? How is the new paradigm for financial markets to be reconciled with the old one? How should financial
markets be regulated? How can the international financial
system be reformed? How can we deal with global warming
and nuclear proliferation? How can we bring about a better
world order? These are the questions for which we have to
find answers. I hope to participate in a lively debate.

Testimony before the U.S. Senate Commerce Committee Oversight Hearing on FTC Advanced Rulemaking on Oil Market Manipulation

Tuesday, June 3, 2008
GEORGE SOROS

Madame Chairperson, distinguished members, I am honored to be invited to testify before your committee. As I understand it, you are seeking an explanation for the recent sharp rise in the oil futures market and in gasoline prices. In particular, you want to know whether this rise constitutes a bubble and, if it is a bubble, whether better regulation could mitigate the harmful consequences.

In trying to answer these questions, I must stress that I am not an expert in oil markets. I have, however, made a life-long study of bubbles. So I will briefly outline my theory of bubbles—which is at odds with the conventional wisdom—and then discuss the current situation in the oil market. I shall focus on financial institutions investing in commodity indexes as an asset class because this is a relatively recent phenomenon and it has become the "elephant in the room" in the futures market.

According to my theory, every bubble has two components: a trend based on reality and a misconception or misinterpretation of that trend. Financial markets are usually very good at correcting misconceptions. But occasionally misconceptions can lead to bubbles because they can reinforce the prevailing trend and by doing so they also reinforce the misconception until the gap between reality and the market's interpretation of reality becomes unsustainable. The misconception is recognized as a misconception, disillusionment sets in, and the trend is reversed. A decline in the value of collaterals provokes margin calls and distress selling causes an overshoot in the opposite direction. The bust tends to be shorter and sharper than the boom that preceded it.

This sequence contradicts the prevailing theory of financial markets, which is based on the belief that markets are always right and deviations from equilibrium occur in a random manner. The various synthetic financial instruments like CDOs and CLOs which have played such an important role in turning the subprime crisis into a much larger financial crisis have been built on that belief. But the prevailing theory is wrong. Deviations can be self-reinforcing. We are currently experiencing the bursting of a housing bubble and, at the same time, a rise in oil and other commodities which has some of the earmarks of a bubble. I believe the two phenomena are connected in what I call a super-bubble that has evolved over the last quarter of a century. The misconception in that super-bubble is that markets tend toward equilibrium and deviations are random.

So much for bubbles in general. With respect to the oil market in particular, I believe there are four major factors at play which mutually reinforce each other.

First, the increasing cost of discovering and developing new reserves and the accelerating depletion of existing oil fields as they age. This goes under the rather misleading name of "peak oil".

Second, there is what may be described as a backward-sloping supply curve. As the price of oil rises, oil-producing countries have less incentive to convert their oil reserves underground, which are expected to appreciate in value, into dollar reserves above ground, which are losing their value. In addition, the high price of oil has allowed political regimes, which are inefficient and hostile to the West, to maintain themselves in power, notably Iran, Venezuela and Russia. Oil production in these countries is declining.

Third, the countries with the fastest growing demand, notably the major oil producers, and China and other Asian exporters, keep domestic energy prices artificially low by providing subsidies. Therefore rising prices do not reduce demand as they would under normal conditions.

Fourth, both trend-following speculation and institutional commodity index buying reinforce the upward pressure on prices. Commodities have become an asset class for institutional investors and they are increasing allocations to that asset class by following an index buying strategy. Recently, spot prices have risen far above the marginal cost of production and far-out, forward contracts have risen much faster than spot prices. Price charts have taken on a parabolic shape which is characteristic of bubbles in the making.

So, is this a bubble? The answer is that the bubble is superimposed on an upward trend in oil prices that has a strong foundation in reality. The first three factors I mentioned are real and would persist even if speculation and commodity index buying were eliminated. In discussing the bubble element I shall focus on institutional buying of commodity indexes as an asset class because it fits so perfectly my theory about bubbles.

Index buying is based on a misconception. Commodity indexes are not a productive use of capital. When the idea was first promoted, there was a rationale for it. Commodity futures were selling at discounts from cash and institutions could pick up additional returns from this so-called "backwardation." Financial institutions were indirectly providing capital to producers who sold their products forward in order to finance production. That was a legitimate investment opportunity. But the field got crowded and that profit opportunity disappeared. Nevertheless, the asset class continues to attract additional investment just because it has turned out to be more profitable than other asset classes. It is a classic case of a misconception that is liable to be self-reinforcing in both directions.

I find commodity index buying eerily reminiscent of a similar craze for portfolio insurance which led to the stock market crash of 1987. In both cases, the institutions are piling in on one side of the market and they have sufficient weight to unbalance it. If the trend were reversed and the institutions as a group headed for the exit as they did in 1987 there would be a crash.

To be sure a crash in the oil market is not imminent. The danger currently comes from the other direction. The rise in oil prices aggravates the prospects for a recession. Only when a recession is well and truly in place is a decline in consumption in the developed world likely to outweigh the other factors I have listed. That makes it desirable to discourage commodity index trading while it is still inflating the bubble.

There is a strong prima facie case against institutional investors pursuing a commodity index buying strategy. It is intellectually unsound, potentially destabilizing and distinctly harmful in its economic consequences.

When it comes to taking any regulatory measures, however, the case is less clear cut. Regulations may have unintended, adverse consequences. For instance, they may push investors further into unregulated markets which are less transparent and offer less protection. It may be possible to persuade institutional investors that they are violating the "prudent man's rule" by acting as a herd just as they did in 1987. If not, buying commodities—as distinct from investing in commodity producing enterprises—should be disqualified as an asset class for ERISA institutions. The various techniques for circumventive speculative position limits should be banned, provided the ban can be made to apply to unregulated as well as regulated markets.

Raising margin requirements would have no effect on the commodity index buying strategy of financial institutions because they use cash. Nevertheless, it would be justified because it would discourage speculation, and speculation can distort prices. Varying margin requirements and minimum reserve requirements are tools that ought to be used more actively to prevent asset bubbles from inflating. This is one of the main lessons to be learned from the recent financial crisis.

Finally, dealing with the bubble element should not divert our attention from the inter-related problems of global warming, energy security and so-called "peak oil". Although they are beyond the scope of these hearings, these are pressing issues that require urgent action.

I hope my remarks are helpful to your deliberations. Thank you.

Paulson Cannot be Allowed a Blank Cheque

Published in the Financial Times *on September 24, 2008*
GEORGE SOROS

Hank Paulson's $700bn rescue package has run into difficulty on Capitol Hill. Rightly so: it was ill-conceived. Congress would be abdicating its responsibility if it gave the Treasury secretary a blank cheque. The bill submitted to Congress even had language in it that would exempt the secretary's decisions from review by any court or administrative agency—the ultimate fulfillment of the Bush administration's dream of a unitary executive.

Mr Paulson's record does not inspire the confidence necessary to give him discretion over $700bn. His actions last week brought on the crisis that makes rescue necessary. On Monday he allowed Lehman Brothers to fail and refused to make government funds available to save AIG. By Tuesday he had to reverse himself and provide an $85bn loan to AIG on punitive terms. The demise of Lehman disrupted the commercial paper market. A large money market fund "broke the buck" and investment banks that relied on the commercial paper market had difficulty financing their operations. By Thursday a run on money market funds was in full swing and we came as close to a meltdown as at any time since the 1930s. Mr Paulson reversed again and proposed a systemic rescue.

Mr Paulson had got a blank cheque from Congress once before. That was to deal with Fannie Mae and Freddie Mac.

His solution landed the housing market in the worst of all worlds: their managements knew that if the blank cheques were filled out they would lose their jobs, so they retrenched and made mortgages more expensive and less available. Within a few weeks the market forced Mr Paulson's hand and he had to take them over.

Mr Paulson's proposal to purchase distressed mortgage-related securities poses a classic problem of asymmetric information. The securities are hard to value but the sellers know more about them than the buyer: in any auction process the Treasury would end up with the dregs. The proposal is also rife with latent conflict of interest issues. Unless the Treasury overpays for the securities, the scheme would not bring relief. But if the scheme is used to bail out insolvent banks, what will the taxpayers get in return?

Barack Obama has outlined four conditions that ought to be imposed: an upside for the taxpayers as well as a downside; a bipartisan board to oversee the process; help for the home-owners as well as the holders of the mortgages; and some limits on the compensation of those who benefit from taxpayers' money. These are the right principles. They could be applied more effectively by capitalising the institutions that are burdened by distressed securities directly rather than by relieving them of the distressed securities.

The injection of government funds would be much less problematic if it were applied to the equity rather than the balance sheet. $700bn in preferred stock with warrants may be sufficient to make up the hole created by the bursting of the housing bubble. By contrast, the addition of $700bn on the demand side of an $11,000bn market may not be sufficient to arrest the decline of housing prices.

Something also needs to be done on the supply side. To prevent housing prices from overshooting on the downside, the number of foreclosures has to be kept to a minimum. The terms of mortgages need to be adjusted to the home-owners' ability to pay.

The rescue package leaves this task undone. Making the necessary modifications is a delicate task rendered more difficult by the fact that many mortgages have been sliced up and repackaged in the form of collateralised debt obligations. The holders of the various slices have conflicting interests. It would take too long to work out the conflicts to include a mortgage modification scheme in the rescue package. The package can, however, prepare the ground by modifying bankruptcy law as it relates to principal residences.

Now that the crisis has been unleashed a large-scale rescue package is probably indispensable to bring it under control. Rebuilding the depleted balance sheets of the banking system is the right way to go. Not every bank deserves to be saved, but the experts at the Federal Reserve, with proper supervision, can be counted on to make the right judgments. Managements that are reluctant to accept the consequences of past mistakes could be penalised by depriving them of the Fed's credit facilities. Making government funds available should also encourage the private sector to participate in recapitalising the banking sector and bringing the financial crisis to a close.

The writer is chairman of Soros Fund Management
Copyright The Financial Times Limited 2008

Recapitalise the Banking System

Published in the Financial Times *on October 2, 2008*
GEORGE SOROS

The emergency legislation before Congress was ill-conceived—or, more accurately, not conceived at all. As Congress tried to improve what Treasury requested, an amalgam plan has emerged that consists of Treasury's original troubled asset relief programme and a quite different capital infusion programme in which the government invests in and stabilises weakened banks and profits from the economy's eventual improvement. The capital infusion approach will cost taxpayers less in future years and may even make money for them.

Two weeks ago the Treasury did not have a plan ready—that is why it had to ask for total discretion in spending the money. But the general idea was to bring relief to the banking system by relieving banks of their toxic securities and parking them in a government-owned fund so that they would not be dumped on the market at distressed prices. With the value of their investments stabilised, banks would then be able to raise equity capital.

The idea was fraught with difficulties. The toxic securities in question are not homogenous and in any auction process the sellers are liable to dump the dregs on to the government fund. Moreover, the scheme addresses only one half of the underlying problem—the lack of credit availability. It does very little to enable house owners to meet their mortgage obligations and it does not address the foreclosure problem. With house prices not yet at the bottom, if the government bids up the price of mortgage-backed securities, the tax-payers are liable to loose; but if the government does not pay up, the banking system does not experience much relief and cannot attract equity capital from the private sector.

A scheme so heavily favouring Wall Street over Main Street was politically unacceptable. It was tweaked by the Democrats, who hold the upper hand, so that it penalises the financial institutions that seek to take advantage of it. The Republicans did not want to be left behind and imposed a re-quirement that the tendered securities should be insured against loss at the expense of the tendering institution. The rescue package as it is now constituted is an amalgam of mul-tiple approaches. There is now a real danger that the asset purchase programme will not be fully utilised because of the onerous conditions attached to it.

Nevertheless, a rescue package was desperately needed and, in spite of its shortcomings, would change the course of events. As late as September 22, Treasury secretary Hank Paulson hoped to avoid using taxpayers' money; that is why he allowed Lehman Brothers to fail. Tarp establishes the principle that public funds are needed and, if the present programme does not work, other programmes will be instituted. We will have crossed the Rubicon. Since Tarp was ill-conceived, it is liable to arouse a negative response from America's creditors. They would see it as an attempt to inflate away the debt. The dollar is liable to come under renewed pressure and the government will have to pay more for its debt, especially at the long end. These adverse consequences could be mitigated by using tax-payers' funds more effectively.

Instead of just purchasing troubled assets the bulk of the funds ought to be used to recapitalise the banking system.

Funds injected at the equity level are more high-powered than funds used at the balance sheet level by a minimal factor of 12—effectively giving the government $8,400bn to re-ignite the flow of credit. In practice, the effect would be even greater because the injection of government funds would also attract private capital. The result would be more economic recovery and the chance for taxpayers to profit from the recovery.

The writer is chairman of Soros Fund Management
Copyright The Financial Times Limited 2008

Acknowledgments

Normally I would circulate my manuscript widely and keep revising it based on the comments I receive. On this occasion I did not have time to do that. Just a few people gave me valuable feedback: Keith Anderson, Jennifer Chun, Leon Cooperman, Martin Eakes, Charles Krusen, John Heimann, Marcel Kasumovich, Richard Katz, Bill McDonough, Pierre Mirabaud, Mark Notturno, Jonathan Soros, Paul Soros, Herb Sturz, Michael Vachon, and Byron Wien. I did receive invaluable assistance on the philosophical part from Colin McGinn, who commented on the text in detail and helped me over some conceptual difficulties. Charles Morris, whose book* I can heartily recommend, understands the intricacies of synthetic financial instruments much better than I do. He and Marcel Kasumovich helped me with the Introduction and Part 2. Raquiba LaBrie and Herb Sturz from my foundation organized a meeting of experts on the foreclosure problem. They along with Solomon Greene and Diana Morris helped with the policy recommendations relating to the subject. Keith Anderson supplied the charts I used in Chapter 5. My publisher, Peter Osnos, and the entire PublicAffairs team

*Charles R. Morris, *The Trillion Dollar Meltdown: Easy Money, High Rollers, and the Great Credit Crash* (New York: PublicAffairs, 2008).

achieved the impossible by publishing the book electronically within a few days of my submitting the final text. Yvonne Sheer and Michael Vachon were as helpful as ever with the entire project. The responsibility for the text is, of course, entirely mine.

Index

About the Author

Sergei Guneyev/SABA

George Soros is chairman of Soros Fund Management and is the founder of a global network of foundations dedicated to supporting open societies. He is the author of several best-selling books, including *The Bubble of American Supremacy*, *Underwriting Democracy*, and *The Age of Fallibility*. He was born in Budapest and lives in New York City.

PublicAffairs is a publishing house founded in 1997. It is a tribute to the standards, values, and flair of three persons who have served as mentors to countless reporters, writers, editors, and book people of all kinds, including me.

I. F. STONE, proprietor of *I. F. Stone's Weekly*, combined a commitment to the First Amendment with entrepreneurial zeal and reporting skill and became one of the great independent journalists in American history. At the age of eighty, Izzy published *The Trial of Socrates*, which was a national bestseller. He wrote the book after he taught himself ancient Greek.

BENJAMIN C. BRADLEE was for nearly thirty years the charismatic editorial leader of *The Washington Post*. It was Ben who gave the *Post* the range and courage to pursue such historic issues as Watergate. He supported his reporters with a tenacity that made them fearless and it is no accident that so many became authors of influential, best-selling books.

ROBERT L. BERNSTEIN, the chief executive of Random House for more than a quarter century, guided one of the nation's premier publishing houses. Bob was personally responsible for many books of political dissent and argument that challenged tyranny around the globe. He is also the founder and longtime chair of Human Rights Watch, one of the most respected human rights organizations in the world.

•   •   •

For fifty years, the banner of Public Affairs Press was carried by its owner Morris B. Schnapper, who published Gandhi, Nasser, Toynbee, Truman, and about 1,500 other authors. In 1983, Schnapper was described by *The Washington Post* as "a redoubtable gadfly." His legacy will endure in the books to come.

Peter Osnos, *Founder and Editor-at-Large*